MOMMY MEMOIRS

What a refreshing view of motherhood! From the early season of diapers and drooling to the process of sending her young men off to their own adventures with a purpose and prayer, Ann Van De Water has captured the essence of motherhood. Enjoy walking through her world with stories that illustrate that armed with a sense of humor and the wisdom of scripture, motherhood is a true joy for those who are brave enough to embark on the journey. Ann's humor is reminiscent of Erma Bombeck and her attitude demonstrates that Christ is the solid rock on which she stands.

—**Krista Schwartzott**, MOPS Coordinator

Ann's book is a "LOL" book! The sincerity about her hectic life as a mother of three boys shows us that it is okay to laugh at ourselves, admit to our imperfections and learn from them...all with God's help. Ann is a role model for other mothers to look up to because she allows Jesus' light to shine through her.

—**Karen H.**, MOPS Coordinator

MOMMY MEMOIRS

A Hilarious and Heartwarming Look at the Trials and Triumphs of Being a Mom!

Ann Van De Water

NEW YORK

MOMMY MEMOIRS
A Hilarious and Heartwarming Look at the Trials and Triumphs of Being a Mom!

Published in New York, New York, by Morgan James Publishing. Morgan James and The Entrepreneurial Publisher are trademarks of Morgan James, LLC. www.MorganJamesPublishing.com

The Morgan James Speakers Group can bring authors to your live event. For more information or to book an event visit The Morgan James Speakers Group at www.TheMorganJamesSpeakersGroup.com.

BitLit
FOR ALL THE BOOKS YOU OWN

FREE eBook edition for your
existing eReader with purchase

_____
PRINT NAME ABOVE

For more information,
instructions, restrictions, and
to register your copy, go to
www.bitlit.ca/readers/register
or use your QR Reader to scan
the barcode:

ISBN 978-1-61448-667-1 paperback
ISBN 978-1-61448-668-8 eBook
ISBN 978 -1-61448-669-5 audio
ISBN 978-1-61448-896-5 hard cover
Library of Congress Control Number:
2013944992

Cover Design by:
Chris Treccani
www.3dogdesign.net

Interior Design by:
Bonnie Bushman
bonnie@caboodlegraphics.com

In an effort to support local communities, raise awareness and funds, Morgan James Publishing donates a percentage of all book sales for the life of each book to Habitat for Humanity Peninsula and Greater Williamsburg.

Get involved today, visit
www.MorganJamesBuilds.com.

Habitat
for Humanity®
Peninsula and
Greater Williamsburg
Building Partner

To my mother and mentor,
Pauline Wipfler,
To my four guys:
My dear husband, Wes,
who is always by my side,
giving me love, encouragement and support,
and to our three sons — Scott, Mark & Ben
who made this mothering adventure such a hoot!
It is a blessing, an honor and a privilege to be your mom.
~Remember ~
no matter how old you get,
you will always be my babies!
May God continue to bless us all.
To Him be the glory!

---

*"A family tree is worth bragging about
if it has consistently produced good timber
and not just nuts!"*
Glen Wheeler

**"Sons are a heritage from the Lord,
children a reward from Him.
Like arrows in the hands of a warrior
are sons born to one's youth."
Psalm 127:3, 4**

CONTENTS

ACKNOWLEDGMENTS

As with any project worth undertaking, there are many hands, eyes, minds and hearts involved in producing the final outcome and this book is no exception. I have many people to thank.

First, I want to thank God for granting me the unbelievable privilege of being the mom of three incredible young men. I thank Him for allowing me to remember my adventures vividly so I could relay them to other moms and encourage you to enjoy and embrace your unforgettable journeys as well.

I also must thank my devoted husband Wes, for his tireless encouragement and support. You planted the seed by asking what I had always wanted to do and once the word "write" was out of my mouth, you were by my side every step of the way as my advisor and personal cheering section. Thank you! I couldn't have completed this book without your unfailing support and unconditional love and I can't imagine life without you!

To my sons, Ben, Mark and Scott for allowing me to tell our stories to the world...that takes courage, maturity and probably a healthy dose of therapy down the road. Thanks for the awesome honor of being your mom. You all make me so proud, it's hard to stay humble. You guys rock!

My dear soul sister Sue McClain, you took the time to painstakingly comb through my manuscript with an eagle eye, to edit and recommend the needed changes before it went to a publisher. You are a mentor and xiv | MOMMY MEMOIRS

dear friend, and I will always treasure our relationship more than you know! Thank you.

I am also extremely grateful to several friends for their inspiring insights as women: Krista Schwartzott, Michelle Borrello, Kristie Rush, Jackie Hanavan and Peg Powers. Your honesty and constructive criticism made this a better book and me a better person. I appreciate all your help!

I would be remiss if I didn't thank my dear brother, John Wipfler, who believed in me even when I didn't believe in myself and helped me launch into the publishing world. I'd also like to thank Terry Whalin, Acquisitions Editor extraordinaire, for agreeing to bring my manuscript before the Publications Board of Morgan James Publishing Company. Thanks for seeing the potential and championing my book! Finally, thanks to David Hancock, Lyza Poulin and Bethany Marshall at Morgan James Publishing as well, for their patience and professionalism.

You all have a very special place in my heart. I thank each of you for partnering with me on this journey and helping me recount my stories with a sense of humor and passionate heart. I am forever grateful.

Introduction

"I WANT TO BE THE PERFECT MOM"

*Whatever you do, do it wholeheartedly as though
you were working for your real master and not merely for humans.
It is Christ, your real master, whom you are serving.
Colossians 3:23-24*

How many of us started on this parenting adventure with the unrealistic, unattainable dream, declaring (if only to ourselves) that we wanted to be the perfect mom? I know I did. Guess what? I wasn't.

This is not intended, by any means, to be a how-to-book. It is more like a "been-there-done-that, fumbled through and by-God's-grace survived!" book. If you glean some golden nugget that will help you in your mothering, it was worth it. To be totally honest, this was intended to be just a work of heart to my four guys (my darling, wonderful husband and our three sons: Scott, Mark, and Ben), a tiny token of my deep appreciation for the rip-roaring ride! It was to be a "thank you" gift of sorts for the years of tears, laughter, heartaches, hilarity, trials and triumphs that marked the coming of age of our boys, the lights of our lives.

If you're waiting to have children until you have your "act together," you might as well forget it. If you're waiting to have kids until you can afford them, then you may be well past the childbearing years before you are financially stable. If you're waiting to have them until you've read all the right books and you know you'll get it all right—here's a news flash! Having children is a labor of love with no instruction manual and the key is saving enough financially to have some money left for your kids' therapy when they are grown.

Yes, I wanted to be the perfect mom. Our intentions are always wonderful. However, life has a way of challenging us all, even on our best days. You know they say that experience is what you get when you don't get what you came for! As is written in one of the following chapters, "It wouldn't have started with something called 'labor' if it was going to be easy." Every mom's sentence is eighteen+ years of hard labor. Moreover, if we do our jobs right, they'll break our hearts and fly from our nests. If we don't do our jobs right, they'll break our hearts, come back to the nest and live at home with us indefinitely!

Seriously, if we play our cards right, we'll reap years of incredible relationships right on down through the generations. What a gift!

I guess everyone has her own idealistic view of how life will be with children: there's Mom in her apron, humming happily as she cooks yet another delicious, lovely, gourmet meal for her model family in a spotless, shiny kitchen. Her older children are playing cheerily in the next room like the best of friends and the baby has been sleeping peacefully upstairs for three hours. Her toddler gurgles contentedly as she hands him a wholesome cracker and her husband comes to the door of their meticulously neat home, with a bouquet of roses in his arms. His darling wife looks pretty as a pin in her wrinkle-free cotton dress, stockings, pumps and makeup that was just touched up. She smells of perfume and rosemary. She winks as she giggles and accepts the roses with a peck on her husband's cheek - a promise of passionate romance after the kids are in bed smelling of baby shampoo and powder. Their dog wags his tail, protects the family valiantly and never once whimpers to be let out to poop! Birds sing in the flower garden that was planted by the industrious, energetic woman of the house. She bakes pies for friends when they have babies, visits and shops for the elderly woman next door on a weekly basis and is the president of the PTA in all her spare time.

Ah! Life as it should be? Could be? Let's try this on for size: it has been pouring all day which means the kids have been underfoot all day. A frazzled mom puts water on to boil for macaroni and cheese and opens a can of green beans as she tries desperately to prevent her two year old from sticking his fingers up the dog's nose. The pet howls and wakes the baby as the older two siblings scream, running through the kitchen chasing each other with light sabers. The doorbell rings and it's the FedEx man needing a signature for a final notice bill from the electric company.

Back inside, the pasta is boiling over and the phone is ringing. It's her mother, reprimanding her for not calling that morning and the toddler has found the dog dish and is eating ALPO. Her husband calls to say he has been delayed at work with an unexpected sales meeting and just as she's about to set the table, her toddler throws up the dog food he ingested onto her old sneakers. She sighs on the verge of tears, then cuts her finger on the green bean can lid and starts to cry in earnest!

A little extreme, but definitely more realistic than the first scenario. Alas, such is life as a mom. It's hectic, it can be depressing at times, and it's exhilarating! It is one adventure after another. None of us can escape the ups and downs, the bumps and bruises—you can count on them. There are the memories that make your heart sing and the moments that shatter your heart into a million aching pieces. It's a journey with many turns and twists. Just remember to be kind to your children along the way; they may someday choose your nursing home!

As in gardening, there will be days of sun and days of rain. If you are lucky, there will only be a little manure, if you catch my drift. The harvest will be abundant if we tend it daily. Our job is to give our children roots that go deep into the soil of a rich heritage. It won't be easy!

I read a job description once about parenting by Victoria Abreo which I thought was very appropriate. Talk about a multitasking, multifaceted job that pays incredible dividends. This one however, will take our breath away if we see it all at once for the supreme effort and energy it will require. We must take on a bit at a time or we will certainly turn the job offer down flat!

If we give all our being to the job, all the roller coaster rides are inevitable. Are they worth it? You bet! It is in giving fully of ourselves that we get more than we ever thought possible. As we love our families with all that's in us, they will return the love in so many different ways and fill us back up. Not every day, but over a lifetime. At least, that's what I found.

I had to write all this down. It is so easy to forget the myriad small details of the days, and then years, as they fly by. Especially in the early stages when your children are just babies; life can be so crazy! You look back and sometimes it's all a blur! (Friends who read this asked, "Did you journal about this as you were living it? How did you remember it all?" I truthfully don't know. I never was a big journal keeper. Nevertheless, the memories poured out of me, clearly and precisely.) I now understand this book to be a gift from God. You'll understand why as you read the pages that follow, especially the chapter about my own mom. I wanted to remember it all because I am not sure how long I will be able to remember. My mom was diagnosed at age 56 with Alzheimer's and the disease has perched as a specter on my shoulder for years.

I know that we all have our own burdens to bear, our own adventures to undertake. However, it makes it so much easier when you know there's someone a few steps ahead that can relate, who has walked the path before you and is willing to share what her life as a mom was all about. Let's open our hearts to walk beside each other as we do this mothering thing. We will be stronger for the journey when we share what we know and admit what we don't know.

So come catch a glimpse of my journey through motherhood, which is far from over. I hope you will understand how important it was to always keep a sense of humor as each day unfolded. Most of all, I hope you see what an honor, privilege and joy I believe it can be to partner with God in one of the most amazing careers you could ever choose. Enjoy a chuckle and perhaps a tear or two. I've been there, done that — and I can honestly say, there is no greater blessing in all my life than being a mom!

—Ann

MY OB-GYN GOES TO MY CHURCH

For You created my inmost being;
You knit me together in my mother's womb.
I praise You because I am fearfully and wonderfully made;
Your works are wonderful, I know that full well.
Psalm 139:13-14

May He give you the desire of your heart,
and make all your plans succeed.
Psalm 20:4

hope you don't mind if I am brutally honest with you. I lived every woman's nightmare! There I was, walking cheerily down the hall of my church on my way to adult Sunday school class with my husband when suddenly I buckled, head down, behind my husband's back. "What the…?" he started to say. I hushed him as I whispered, "Just keep going, please!"

We were new in the area and I had randomly chosen, for the sake of convenience, an OB-GYN office in my home town. I had never had the pleasure of "being seen" by a gynecologist in high school or even college. ("Hi, I'm Dr. Seymour Yu, at your cervix!") I figured if all the plumbing and fixtures were working, why see a plumber? I did start to see a doctor when my husband and I started experiencing trouble conceiving and was assured that everything was indeed in working order, so to speak. Nevertheless, it was a trip I foolishly put off as long as I could.

I was mortified, but strangely excited at the same time about going to my first appointment with an OB when I realized I was finally pregnant after trying for over four years to have a baby. Granted, I had to pay him to see me naked, but suddenly it all seemed so much more acceptable, being on the table, since I was "doing it for the baby!"

However, I never anticipated the jolt of that Sunday morning. "That's my OB-GYN!" I whispered carefully after he was out of earshot. "Oh-my-gosh! I can't believe he goes here! You don't suppose he recognized me…since I'm dressed! Do you think?"

Flash forward: I had a nightmare a month later: I dreamt that his office was in our church and they put a reminder of my annual in the bulletin one Sunday. The head usher was the receptionist and the worship team sang praises when my mammogram came back normal. Am I normal? Does every woman go through these kinds of anxiety issues? I think I'm going to be excommunicated!

Now, almost three decades later, I half expect him to greet me in the hall with, "Hi Ann! Now that you're going through the change, I hope you tithed this morning."

He would never! He's the consummate professional. I have to admit that I still hurry past him with a quick hello, despite the fact that he had a hand (literally) in delivering all three of our sons.

So began my incredible journey into motherhood and all the embarrassing, exhilarating, heartbreaking, hilarious moments it would entail over the next twenty-five plus years. Every woman's journey is different, but all have similarities. You can never gather women in the same room without the conversation eventually turning to pregnancies, deliveries and the raising of their children. How could you? It is all consuming — as it should be. What other job is more important in all of creation than the one of partnering with God to create and nurture another human being, made in His image?

Yes, our lives become one long "I'm doing it for the baby!" and they continue to be your "baby" no matter how old they get. Our mother instincts are tuned at every turn, waiting to protect, nurture, encourage, fix…we can't help it. That's the way God designed us. It's what we were made for. Let's celebrate it!

BRAXTON HICKS:
IS THAT A DEPARTMENT STORE?

Being confident of this,
that He who began a good work in you
will carry it on to completion...
Philippians 1:6

Always give yourselves fully to the work of the Lord;
Because you know that your labor in the Lord is not in vain.
1 Corinthians 15:58

I've always loved talking to younger women about childbearing. It just cracks me up. Truth be known, I was none the wiser in the ways of obstetrics and all that meant before I was in the "family way." You don't get it, unless you've been through it. Talk to any mom who braved the nine+/- months of pregnancy and inevitably, she has her own tale to tell about her experience. Most of us experience some amount of "Braxton Hicks" contractions, which is the official term for *false labor*. For some of us, our actual experiences with the real deal delivery are humorous, some are horrifying (love the deliveries in elevators and taxis) and some are relatively boring and humdrum. It never ceases to amaze me when I hear of women in days gone by, giving birth in some field, wrapping up the new arrival and continuing with their labors (no pun intended!)

As I said before, each tale is different, yet similar. We're all meant to have a gestation period of about nine months…give or take. Many of us "train" to deliver naturally. Some of us "strain" to deliver naturally, yet never get the chance to do so. Some go through hours and hours of labor, which to us feel like days, only to end up in a C-section. Yours truly! Others waltz in as if it's another stop in their busy day and push that little sucker out like nobody's business in less time than it takes to bake a cake!

All three of my babies were C-sections after more than a full day of labor! The first, all nine pounds three ounces of him, wouldn't fit through my narrow pelvis. C-section! The second was conveniently scheduled before my doctor was due on the green for his golf date. C-section! I tried to deliver my third naturally, was given an epidural and ended up hurling the whole time he was being born…C-section! Thank God I was not a frontier woman.

I never did understand why they didn't put a zipper in, as I recommended after my first. It would have been so much more convenient, wouldn't you think? Alas, I am no doctor. However, if you want to make millions, figure out a way to do that!

So — Braxton Hicks? Must have been two guys, Braxton & Hicks, that needed each other to help figure out it was false labor. In other words, "Go home." To a first time mother like me, those two words can be devastating. I geared up emotionally, psychologically, physically, and mentally to deliver this baby and then was told, "Go home!" So I sat on my front porch and my friends yelled from their car windows, "You're still pregnant?" Yes! Thank you very much!

Braxton Hicks? I wish it was a department store. I'd ask to speak to the management to log a formal complaint: "No more fooling around. It's been nine months. Get this baby out of me!"

CABBAGE ROLLS AND COMEDIES

For we are God's fellow workers...
1 Corinthians 3:9

A woman giving birth to a child has pain
because her time has come;
but when her baby is born she forgets the anguish
because of her joy that a child is born into the world.
John 16:21

had always heard that if you want to get your labor started you should drive on bumpy, hilly roads to speed up the onset of contractions. We tried that. It didn't work. What really worked well was a dinner of cabbage rolls and a trip to the movie theater to watch a comedy and laugh heartily.

I remember a picture of me, taken the day I went into labor for real, standing on the shore of Lake Erie with my hands resting on my huge, very pregnant belly. By the end of my pregnancy, I could balance a glass of iced tea on that bulge. It was very impressive. I had edema (a condition where you retain water) and I recall pressing my finger into the top of my feet which looked like blown up surgical gloves and having the dimple last for several minutes. It really grossed out our friends, especially the ones who weren't parents yet and had never experienced the joys of pregnancy. So, I went home from our afternoon at the shore wondering…was it really time?

Of course, being the first time that I had ever experienced real labor, and having endured the humiliation of a Braxton Hicks false alarm two weeks earlier, I was reticent to believe this was the real deal when things got going. It's gas. The cabbage rolls are finally digesting and this pain I'm feeling will dissipate, won't it? All that laughing in the theater just made me sore.

Well, by the time we got to the hospital my husband, like most husbands, was a basket case. However, after the initial shock of "Oh my gosh, my wife's really having our baby this time!" he got right down to business. He was a trooper — even when I dug my nails into his forearms and cursed his very existence for putting me in this condition. We could laugh about it later…much later! The miracle of it all was that we even contemplated having more children after it was all over, though it took over thirty hours in every case to finally welcome each of our boys into the world.

God does an amazing thing for us women, doesn't He? He helps us forget the misery and outrageous pain of labor and delivery once we hold that precious tiny bundle in our arms. I read once that, "Children are God's message that the world should go on." Sometimes, when things seem sad and spiraling out of control, I hang on to that thought. Somehow, I have forgotten just how difficult my deliveries were because I have been so blessed! I thank God for my three sons who give me purpose, focus and untold joy.

Will this be the day?

Two more months,
really?

I'm wearing blue,
does that mean anything?

LOOK AT THE MESS YOU MADE

L ook at the mess you made! Makes me think of a cartoon I saw once. It was a picture of a baby chick that had just broken out of its shell, looking very remorseful as the mother hen was yelling "Now look what you did!" Like it had a choice. I could relate to that little chick!

I had to pace. I paced and paced and breathed deeply and held my abdomen, sure I would be delivering a baby elephant with the pressure I felt. To relieve the severity of the contractions, I paced around the bed, shaking off my poor husband who asked repeatedly, "Is there anything I can do?" "Yes," I answered, exasperatedly, "deliver this baby for me, will you please, because right about now, I don't really want to do this and I can't believe this is all your fault and why didn't you talk me out of this because I'm not sure at all now that I even want to be a mother and yes, let's just trade places and you can lie on the bed and drop a bowling ball out of your body, how does that sound?"

Just then, I heard another woman scream bloody murder down the hall. Being a first timer - I thought for sure that baby must have weighed in at a whopping fifty pounds by the sound penetrating every bone in my already weary body and that mother was dying as she gave life. Honestly, I was "fragile" at this point. Then it happened.

They tell you that if this occurs in the grocery store to grab a jar of pickles and throw it on the floor...no one will know that your water broke but you! Of course, with my luck, I'd be in the produce aisle. It kind of loses its effectiveness when you toss down a green pepper or head of broccoli.

Anyway, in comes "Nurse Nasty" who takes one look at me, drops her eyes to the floor and sneers through pursed lips, "Look at the mess you made!" Now I'm not normally in the habit of biting people's heads off, but in my current "fragile" state, I would have made a tasty snack of Nurse Nasty if it hadn't been for the next contraction which took my breath away. Nurse Nasty lucked out. She grabbed a mop, cleaned up my *mess* and stomped out of the room.

Then there was the perky young aide who bounded in the morning after my C-section and gaily announced, "Upsy daisy, I'm making your bed." Grabbing me by both arms, she yanked me up and quite honestly, I don't remember what happened after that. I think the screams I heard were from me this time and then, all hell broke loose as nurses came running from everywhere. Maybe "Miss Perky" was responsible for the scream I heard the night before. I hope she's found a new position as a secretary in an accounting firm. I think the OB in this hospital stood for oblivious, obtrusive, and obnoxious, or maybe "OB-surd." Amazingly, my surgical stitches stayed intact!

WHAT, NO INSTRUCTION MANUAL?

It doesn't seem right. Every toy that we have ever bought, every appliance that is on the market, every piece of equipment available from department stores all over this great nation of ours comes, not only with a 90 day money back guarantee, but a service agreement and a lengthy instruction manual that takes a rocket scientist to figure out. There are a gazillion steps with pictures and arrows and instructions that sound like a foreign language when you read them out loud.

With a baby, zip, zilch, zero, nothing, nil, nada! I still can't believe I was allowed to leave the hospital with this newborn in my arms with no training whatsoever! As parents, we're supposed to figure everything out for ourselves; from how to feed them and burp them, to how to diaper them and get them to go to sleep. We are not told what to do if their umbilical cord doesn't fall off when it is supposed to. What should we do when they suck in their lower lip each time they inhale? Should we worry? Is it asthma? How does one prevent hair loss that turns their infant into a combination of monk and Mohican when they nurse? How does a parent survive colic? Why on earth would they suck on their own toes? We have no instructions for what to do when they won't eat the gross, green slimy stuff in the baby food jar, and spit it out all over our trying-hard-to-smile faces!

How about when they have the habit of taking off their diaper and running around naked when you have dinner guests? Should we nurture their artistic tendencies when they draw on the walls with their poop? When will they outgrow the urge to flush everything (including the pet hamster) down the toilet? Should we worry if they eat or drink out of the dog dish? How do we stop our little girls from lifting up their dresses when the children's choir is singing? How do we teach our boys that picking their noses during school concerts isn't appropriate? How can we stop them from biting the neighbor kid or worse yet, the neighbor's dog! What if they curse before they talk? What if they shimmy before they walk? Should I worry if my child asks for a cell phone at the ripe age of three? What if the teacher calls to report that Junior was caught smooching in the kindergarten cubby? Do I home school until he's eighteen? *How* do you discipline when you're trying very hard not to burst out in peals of laughter?

We parents should demand an instruction manual! We could really use the pictures, the arrows and even the extended factory warranty. No return policy is necessary. We would never want to give them back. Maybe what we need is an instruction manual written by moms and dads. Now there's an idea! Watch for it!

HE IS SO A NEWBORN

I prayed for this child
and the Lord has granted me what I asked of him.
So now I give him to the Lord.
1 Samuel 1:27-28

sn't it wonderful going to the newborn nursery window in a hospital and looking down at all those little pink and blue bundles? Some are sleeping peacefully, while others are yelling their little lungs out to complain about hunger pangs or perhaps wet diapers. Most of them look like wrinkled old men, especially when they are letting loose with a robust, full-blown cry! Some have been given names, yet others are only identified as "Baby Last Name" but you can tell the parents with their noses pressed against the glass, beaming proudly as the nurses hold up their bellowing infant to receive appropriate oohs and aahs from adoring relatives.

After some thirty+ hours of labor and delivery, and a C-section to end it all, I shuffled down to the window in a moment of restlessness because I couldn't wait to see my baby again. My doctor had said the more I got out of my room, the faster I'd get out of the hospital. There is no denying the telltale waddle of a C-section Mom, as I held my abdomen to prevent the stitches from bursting open and my guts from gushing out, which I was sure would happen any moment. I made my way, inch by inch, down the maternity ward hallway in my double layer "modest" hospital gown, with the nursing stains giving yet another hint as to my identity.

Scotty looked like a little Eskimo baby. He had a full head of dark black hair that stood up on end covering a beautifully shaped, round head (a sign of being lifted out of the womb versus pushing through the birth canal). I was in no shape (literally) to deliver him naturally. My pelvis and his head were not compatible. So, I was rushed into surgery for my first C-section as his heart rate plummeted with each contraction.

Despite my puffy, worn out appearance, I had to swallow my female pride and drag myself down for a peek. As I stood there, ogling my newborn, one of the other admirers pointed at my son and said, "That one can't be a newborn! He's huge and he's absolutely beautiful!" I cleared my throat and shyly admitted, "On the contrary, he most definitely is a newborn and I have the stitches to prove it!" We all had a good laugh, and of course, the other new mom and I compared notes on our deliveries before I started to feel the exhaustion of my journey down the hall and had to excuse myself to shuffle back to my room.

Now, I have the smiley scar to prove that I had three C-sections, and I wear it proudly! In retrospect, as hard as each delivery was, that was the easy part. Raising these sons well for God was the harder thing! It was a decision I had to make everyday at every turn. Truthfully, some days I forgot to give them to God. In my arrogance, I thought I could do it in my own strength. Boy, was I wrong!

All that black hair and I never had any heartburn; so much for old wives' tales!

BAWLING WITH THE BABY

Come to me, all you who are weary and burdened
and I will give you rest.
Matthew 11:28

W hy is it that when you take a baby home, you expect that everything will be hunky-dory; baby will sleep, you will sleep and everyone will live happily ever after. We had never even heard the word *colic* before we had our first. Maybe that's one of those taboo words that all the nurses in the maternity ward are told never to utter. "Oh dear, I think this baby has…you know…the 'C' word, but don't tell the parents, whatever you do! They'll know soon enough." They would nod knowingly to each other and saunter off to do their nursery duties, leaving us in the dark, totally oblivious about the dark days to come.

No one really knows what causes colic. Dorland's Medical Dictionary defines it as "benign paroxysmal abdominal pain during the first three months of life." Of course it doesn't say whether those symptoms are experienced by the parents or the baby. Ours seemed to last more like three years! All we remember is standing in the middle of the nursery with our newborn in our arms, crying just as loudly as him. My husband and I would pass him back and forth during the wee hours of the morning, jostling, bouncing, cajoling, swaying and bawling right along with him because we were so damn tired! We went through our days on auto pilot, cursing parenthood and swearing we were not going to do this ever again!

Scotty would draw his legs up and scream for hours on end. Being a novice at nursing, I was insecure and sure my milk was "bad" for him. However, the pediatrician assured us that he was growing bigger, stronger and healthier by the day. We could tell he was indeed healthy — he had lungs to challenge Luciano Pavarotti at 3:00 in the morning. His thighs had four rolls, so pinch-able you couldn't resist. He wasn't so adorable though when he screamed his head off for two hours straight before dawn, only to finally settle down just before we had to get up and going for the day!

We really don't remember very much from our first few months of parenthood. It all passed by in a blur, with us floundering in the dense fog of sleep deprivation. Finally, when it began to dissipate, we would awaken in a panic and check to be sure he was okay—mostly out of habit, just to reassure ourselves that he was indeed still breathing in his crib. Then one day, we looked at each other and realized we had survived. Before we knew it, we were pregnant again with baby #2. It had taken years to get pregnant and lo and behold, twenty-one months after Scott, along came Mark. God does have a sense of humor. Boy, were we busy!

Wes and I realized through all this that our friends who said they slept like babies didn't have any yet! "Come to me all who are weary and burdened and I will give you rest." Wow, did that sound good. It still does today! We thought once they were grown, we would be able to relax. Not so much!

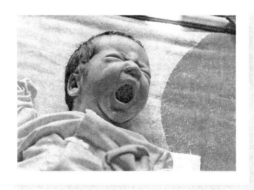

How is it possible for him to still be so darn cute?

AFTERNOON DELIGHT OR NOT

Let him kiss me with the kisses of his mouth -
for your love is more delightful than wine.
Take me away with you - let us hurry!
Let the king bring me into his chambers.
Song of Songs 1:2, 4

Love is the duty of the present moment.
Jean Pierre DeCaussade

One of the things we noticed when we first became parents were the limited opportunities we had for intimacy. Suddenly our lives were consumed with feedings and diaper changes and baths and more diaper changes and more feedings. Before we knew it, we were dropping into bed, exhausted with literally nothing to give to each other at the end of the day. Especially after nights of being awake a good amount of the time, either nursing or dealing with colic, the last thing on my mind was "love!"

One afternoon we surprised ourselves and realized we were "in the mood" at the same time with a little extra energy to devote to one another. We had just put our little angel down for his afternoon nap an hour before so we thought we would take advantage of the quiet in the house, gaze into each other's eyes and see what developed. Feeling hungry for the physical togetherness we had denied ourselves for what seemed to be an eternity, we jumped under the covers and sighed deep sighs of contentment.

All was as it should be. Our little boy was fast asleep, we were deeply in love and we had what we thought would be a chunk of time to enjoy some closeness for a change. Our energies were focused on each other instead of our new baby for the first time in a long time and we were thrilled!

Now before I give away the ending of the story, you have to understand the layout of our house. The second story of our home at the time consisted of three bedrooms and a tiny office in a square off of a small hall, with the bathroom at the top of the square and the stairs heading down to the main floor opposite the bathroom. The nursery was kitty-corner to our master bedroom. The way we had decorated the nursery situated the crib on the wall of the hall with one inch to spare at the doorway. Our queen sized bed had a clear view of the nursery doorway. We meant it to be that way so we could leave doors open and easily check in to be sure all was well. We didn't think of course that the reverse was also true.

So here we were, enjoying some afternoon delight when suddenly we heard a little voice from across the hall say, "Hi!" We froze and when I glanced with horror over my shoulder, (they say position is everything in life) there was our son's cheery cherub face, straining around the

"Peek-a-boo, I see you!"

doorframe to observe the goings-on in the master bedroom. We don't think he is permanently scarred, but we're not sure. We rearranged the master bedroom that afternoon!

SMACK HIM AGAIN
AND PUT HIM BACK

Then the Lord said to Cain, "Where is Abel?"
"I don't know," he replied. "Am I my brother's keeper?"
Genesis 4:9

love to tell the joke about the little girl whose mother was in labor and about to deliver. Between contractions, the laboring mom asked her daughter to call 911 and soon there was an EMT at the door asking where Mom was, and giving little Abbey instructions on how to help him deliver the baby. Abbey did as she was told and was a great help. Soon she had a new baby brother and Mom was just fine.

After spanking the baby and getting him to cry, the EMT handed baby Aaron over to Mom. Then he turned and asked Abbey what she thought of the whole experience. Abbey put her hands on her hips, pursed her lips and exclaimed, "Smack him again. He shouldn't have crawled up there in the first place!"

The earliest picture we have of bringing our second baby, Mark, home is a photo of me, holding Mark with a very tearful big brother pointing at the front door. I had had my second C-section, so I couldn't pick up Scotty for quite a while and it broke his heart. He didn't understand and saw Mark as the reason I couldn't "love" him. His response to seeing the new addition to the family was a definitive "Put him back!"

It is truly amazing that sibling rivalry doesn't take more of a toll in the grand scheme of things. Of course, no mom would ever wish to put their baby back - despite the days we wish someone would take junior off our hands! It can be a daunting task, especially when you already have one, two or more ankle-biters at home vying for your attention every minute of every hour of the day. Families that have girls first often have the bonus of a second little "mommy" to help with the newborn when they arrive. Daughters just have that inborn nature to nurture and most want to be "Mommy's little helper" any chance they get.

I know of a family with eight children - God bless this mother who also home-schools her flock. The family is amazing. The oldest two of the eight are girls, the next four are all boys and the last one, another girl, is on the way. The daughters are getting such incredible experiences at being mothers, watching their younger brothers frequently for their very busy mom and helping around the house with chores. They will be awesome moms when they have their own children. The boys are still young but my guess is that they will be too busy with their rough and tumble activities to bother much with a new baby. I may be wrong.

Don't *get* me wrong, however! The gender roles are not exclusive. The environment in their home is one of helping out and all of them, little guys included, know their responsibilities: waking at dawn to milk

" I asked for a puppy!
Put him back!"

the cows, feed the goats, vacuum the den or set the table for a big family breakfast before their lessons begin. They are a farming family and I have the utmost respect for the home life they have created.

God has blessed this family with a house-full of children and a home full of love. I'm sure no one would vote to put anyone back, although they probably all get their ration of healthy light smacks (as well as healthy light snacks) now and then! Didn't we all?

I HAVE A HEGG-ACHE

*Train a child in the way he should go and when he is old
he will not turn from it.*
Proverbs 22:6

I don't know when the genes come into play that determine a child's "bent." Will they be musically talented or headed onto the stage, scientifically astute, mathematically brilliant or artistically inclined? All I know is that some of these signs can show up at a fairly young age.

We wanted to train our boys to clean up after playtime so they realized that making messes and leaving them was not acceptable. We weren't always successful! Consequently, after spreading toys all over the den floor and observing that the boys randomly played with maybe three of them, I determined it was time for clean up. We were nearing the crunch hour — when both boys and mom needed a nap!

Many times we made it a game: who can clean up the most toys the fastest? Who can figure out which toy mommy has behind her back that needs to be put away? Of course, their idea of clean was rarely my idea of clean and one of the toughest things I had to learn was accepting what they had made the effort to do.

So, back to the genes; I know I had a tendency when I was little to be a drama queen, loving high-heeled shoes and dress-up, begging to put on shows for Mom and the neighborhood, and being very dramatic about life. My mother used to say that I lived my life on the hilltops or in the valleys. Not a lot about my childhood was even keeled. Life was either great: full of sunshine and flowers, or the end of the world: dark, dismal and full of tragedy. I would either be singing or crying — that's just how it was.

Well, along came my boys and I remember calling my mother on the phone and complaining about something dramatic or traumatic that had occurred. Mom would just chuckle softly and say, "There is justice! History repeats itself!" She could totally relate. I had given her fits.

So when I clapped my hands and announced that it was time to clean up the toys, did my boys jump to attention and begin the white tornado organization of their belongings to please their mother and make my life rosy? In my dreams, yes! In reality, Scott would put his hand up onto his forehead and with a serious, dramatic exhalation he would exclaim, "Not now Mommy. I have a hegg-ache!" at which point my four year old would sink to the floor and hold his head in his hands as if it would explode any minute.

Drama. Does it get carried in the genes? Is the propensity for the hills and valleys of life passed on from generation to generation? Nature versus nurture has been an age-old debate. However, scares me how much our kids can pick up from us when we are least aware. There's not a great deal that gets past them. I know I've said, "Not now dear, I have a headache" on more than one occasion. Was Scott listening? He's watched us; he certainly could have heard us.

A FOREHEAD EMBEDDED
WITH BROCCOLI

Don't be fools; be wise;
make the most of every opportunity for doing good.
Ephesians 5:16

Sometimes, as new parents, we forget that we have a little one, or two, to consider in our social life. We can't seem to let go of the fun we had as "DINKS" (double income / no kids) so we pack our engagement calendar full of get-togethers: drinks or dinners out with friends, thinking we will just bring Junior along since they're in a nip-nap and very transportable. They'll just hang out in their rocker seat while we yuck it up with our DINK friends and they will be no worse for the wear.

That did work for a little while. Since babies spend so much time napping in the beginning, it can actually work out quite nicely. We managed well in the first few months of parenthood, still entertaining and being entertained with our little "Porta-Scotty"! Then Mark came along and things got a little trickier. At that point, Scott was mobile and energetic; we couldn't get him to sit down for very long at all. So, enjoying a cup of coffee or glass of iced tea with friends became quite a challenge. It is amazing when you visit friends who don't have children, how much trouble your kids can get into in a house that is not childproofed.

We had pushed our two little boys one day with a Lawn and Garden Show for a few hours at a Convention Center and then enjoyed snacks at a restaurant nearby with some friends. When we finally got home that evening to make and eat dinner, our Scott was absolutely exhausted. He was so tired, he didn't even "crash and burn" — (our term when the boys caused a scene because we had not ended the fun soon enough.)

We came home and put Mark up in his crib. We made dinner and sat down to eat. Scott's eyes were rolling back in his head and he was trying valiantly to stay awake. Every now and then, his eyes would close and his head would bob down until he jerked back awake and lamely lifted his spoon up. Rarely did it make it into his mouth, he didn't have the strength! He sat there in his highchair listlessly. Finally with one last ditch effort to take in some food, his head fell forward and smashed down into his plate of chicken and broccoli with a resounding whack, where it stayed until we rushed over to lift his face out of his dinner. He was fast asleep! There, embedded on his forehead were little broccoli florets that stuck on his skin with the force of his face-down boogie! Poor little guy. We had pushed him beyond his limit.

How often do we go out to restaurants or malls, for example, and hear parents reprimanding their children or trying to corral them as they dive under the table, because they are in the "crash and burn" stage? Are we having fun yet?

A LIGHT SNACK AND IPECAC

I t takes but a second. It's happened to most of us parents. You look away for just a moment and something happens with your child that you never anticipated. It could be as inconsequential as tripping and skinning a knee, or as tragic as losing your little one to drowning. We've all experienced it to some degree or another. Luckily for us, it was the former. Inconsequential, no big deal — though at the time, we didn't know how it would turn out.

It is said that mushrooms, the poisonous kind, can lead to all sorts of ailments and even death, if ingested. A dramatic range of symptoms can occur from mild stomachache to severe physical distress including vomiting, diarrhea, cramps, loss of coordination, hallucination and even death. We knew of the possible ramifications of eating unknown varieties and we couldn't take any chances.

When Scott was just a toddler, we were chatting with some friends who had stopped by to chat as we enjoyed a sunny day on our front lawn. We were all engrossed in our conversation when Wes realized that Scotty had bent down, picked something out of the grass and put it in his mouth. When Wes inspected the situation further, we found remnants of a mushroom in Scott's tightly clenched little fist. He was very reticent to give it up and even more stubborn about opening his mouth. We were finally able to pry open his teeth to remove the pieces of mushroom we could see that Scott hadn't swallowed, so we quickly placed them in a baggie and sped off to the emergency room.

We explained the situation breathlessly as the nurse ushered us into one of the examining rooms and took Scotty's vitals. He was not at all happy about the whole situation. They took the evidence in the plastic bag and sent it to a lab. By the time they finally saw Scott and gave him Ipecac, he would have probably suffered any or all the symptoms. It seemed like forever! Of course, as a parent, fifteen minutes seems like forever when you are faced with a possibly life-threatening situation!

Ipecac is a very effective drug. Within seconds, Scotty had emptied his stomach of everything he had eaten that day and then some. It turned out that the mushroom was not poisonous and the violent vomiting brought on by the Ipecac was for nothing. However, we couldn't risk it.

To this day, Scott loves mushrooms, though he opts wisely for the store-bought variety.

If you glance away for even a moment, they'll always get into trouble! Marky-Dano!

THE COUSINS AND
THE CORNMEAL

T hey say that parents have a sixth sense when something is wrong. Don't ask them how they know, they just do. Like when everything gets strangely quiet all of a sudden, and your heart leaps into your throat because you realize you haven't seen your child for a little too long and you have no idea where they are.

There is nothing more terrifying than experiencing that feeling in a store as you are shopping. The sudden realization that your child is not by your side is as terrifying an experience as you could ever have as a parent. No matter how attentive you are, there will come a time when you're distracted and you lose sight of your little shopper. It is a situation I wouldn't wish on any mom. Obviously the outcome can be tragic.

I remember when our boys were little and prone to wander or run amuck, there was a product on the market which became quite fashionable. It was two Velcro wristbands attached by a plastic coil, like a telephone cord. The idea was to attach one end on your child's wrist and the other on yours so they could not escape when you were out in public. It was especially handy when you shopped and really convenient when you had an infant in a stroller and a two-year-old who wanted to cruise. Of course, it felt strangely similar to walking the dog, but as young parents we brushed off that awkward thought and used these regularly.

Granted, your child can disappear in the confines of your own home as well and give you a fright. You never know what they'll get into: flushing GI Joes down the toilet, trying on Mom's makeup or perfumes, drawing on the new wallpaper in the bedroom, putting the cat in the dryer, going fishing in the aquarium, feeding the dog PlayDoh…oh the list is endless. There it is again — that eerie feeling that something is not right. It's just too quiet and the little rascals are nowhere to be seen.

We had lost track of Scott and his cousin Matthew one day during a visit on the Cape when they were about eighteen months old. We were catching up with Matt's parents in a delicious moment of relaxation, confessing our blunders as new parents when everything grew very quiet and we panicked to find our boys missing. Everyone jumped up from their seats and scattered, looking for the two cousins in every corner of the house. One of us turned the corner into the kitchen to find the boys covered in cornmeal, having the time of their lives as they drew with fingers on the dusty floor and patted their cornmeal covered hair with pudgy hands. It was a relief to find no harm done and we laughed ourselves silly with relief and pulled out the cameras. However, we learned an important lesson that day: silence is not always golden!

"This is more fun
than finger painting!"

YOU HAVEN'T LIVED
UNTIL YOU'VE EXPERIENCED
PROJECTILE VOMITING

always wondered what they meant when people would say, "Wow, he is the spitting image of you!" Now I know.

Yes, we are talking Olympic caliber hurling that reaches the wall when you're standing, cradling a distraught baby in the middle of a twelve-by-twelve master bedroom at three in the morning. Then again, there is just something about that smell, at that hour, which could get you doing the same!

Mark was not a big baby, but you would have thought that he was a nineteen year old college student who'd had too much to drink! He never had colic, thank God, but he could heave with the best of them and go on with his business, not bothered in the least by the interruption. At first we were absolutely horrified, not knowing if this symptom of digestive distress was a portent of even worse things to come. However, our pediatrician calmly informed us that he would outgrow it, and there was really no reason to worry. That was little consolation to gagging parents cleaning up the mess in the wee hours. Mark continued to gain weight which proved the doctor right again.

That was nothing compared to our experience of rushing him into the hospital, listless and blazing hot. We didn't know how to stop the diarrhea or drop the fever, after our efforts with the B.R.A.T. diet failed (**b**ananas, **r**ice, **a**pplesauce and **t**oast to lessen diarrhea) and the cool bath did little to reduce his temperature. It was heartbreaking to see him all hooked up to intravenous lines, laying there very still, when we were so accustomed to the energy, laughter and smiles of a very active eight year old. Luckily, he was only dehydrated, and soon the IVs took hold. For any parent, it is a scare that takes your breath away and has you praying fervently for some good news to hold your worries at bay.

In retrospect, we were unbelievably fortunate with our three sons. Despite their boyish risks, mischievous schemes and immortal attitudes growing up, we never had any true, life threatening emergencies. They did know guys who bled on sledding hills, drank, did drugs, buried hatchets into their shins, or ate suicide Buffalo chicken wings to the point of being rushed to the ER with gastritis! None of our three got hurt even when they linked hundreds of rubber bands to make a mega-human-slingshot and catapulted Ben up into the air or shot baby doll heads across our backyard pond with bottle rockets. We were indeed fortunate when we stopped them from launching rocks off our roof and into our pond and themselves off our roof and into our pool. I'm the only one in the family that ever broke a bone! (Go figure! The only female in the family.)

I know the boys had guardian angels working overtime. The angels earned extra for their meticulous care of our three. They definitely racked up frequent flyer miles if they didn't earn their wings outright! I know I've heard bells on many occasions.

MARKY ATE IT

Proof of the Existence of Original Sin

Confess your faults one to another and pray one for another.
James 5:16

I think Scott must have been just under three and Mark was a couple of months old, still nursing and in a nip-nap or propped in a laundry basket filled with toys which I often placed on the kitchen counter as I busied myself with making dinner. Scott would play at my feet with our Tupperware collection that we kept very accessible in a cupboard on ground level. He loved to build towers out of the containers and knock them down. Sometimes I would prop him on a chair and fill the kitchen sink with water. Then I would load in everything I could think of to measure and pour and suck and squirt the water. Now and then I'd get brave and include dish soap so that bubbles would also be part of the entertainment. It was a great way to keep Scott nearby and out of trouble.

One evening, he had chosen to play with trucks and cars on the den floor which was just a couple of steps down from the kitchen and eating area. There was a railing and then the sunken den which had a fireplace and mantel. The floor was hardwood so it was perfect for racing and crashing cars and trucks which we collected like it was our job. After

Mark came along, two or more toy trucks or cars were at the bottom of every Christmas stocking for years.

As I cooked, I would glance over to make sure everything was fine. At one point in the casserole-making process, I had grated some cheese over the top of the casserole and set the little bit that was left on the counter. Scott had a nose for cheese — he loved it as a snack, and before too long, I saw him drop what he was doing and head up the three stairs from the den into the kitchen. He hauled a chair over to the counter on the opposite side from where I was digging into the fridge and set his plan in motion. Suddenly, a little pudgy hand stretched up, feeling along on the countertop for the unused portion of cheese. He patted his hand across until he felt it and his fist swiftly disappeared, clutching the tiny morsel. I chuckled to myself and decided to play along.

"Scotty, where is the cheese that Mommy was using to make dinner? It was on the counter and now I can't find it."

"Marky ate it!" he answered.

I couldn't believe it! Mark was still nursing with just a slight start on baby food! It astounded me that Scott would come up so quickly with a lie to cover his theft. It was probably the first teachable moment in his tender young life. I told him I knew he had lied. He was at once remorseful and opened his clenched fist to show me a melted glob of cheese. He apologized and I let him gobble it up. "Say cheese" had a whole new meaning after that.

Bubble trouble, keeping big
brother entertained

Tupperware in the cupboard...
baby in the cupboard!

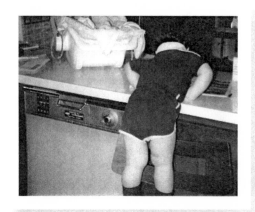

"I know there's cheese
around here somewhere!

DO WORMS HAVE TONSILS?

and Other Earth Shattering Questions

When I was a child, I talked like a child,
I thought like a child, I reasoned like a child.
1 Corinthians 13:11

How is it that kids come up with the most wonderfully innocent questions that can be brilliant and silly at the same time? Sometimes their questions give us glimpses into their amazing brains, working overtime to take in the great expanse of their growing world. Sometimes they're just plain ridiculous, but you've gotta love 'em!

My mom told me that when I was little I asked, "Who holds your head while God screws in your arms?" Now *that* was a great question. I'm not sure how she answered, but I'm sure she got a heartwarming chuckle out of it!

Our boys asked awesome questions like: "Do worms have tonsils?" and "Does baloney have seeds?" Quite honestly, mothers today have an incredible advantage because they can run to their computers or pull out their Smartphones and plug a vital question into Google Search and come back sounding very impressive and knowledgeable. I'm not sure how intelligently I responded to either of those two questions, but my sons seemed quite satisfied at the time with whatever I told them. I could tell they were maturing when they started asking questions that really had answers.

Some answers are no-brainers, others take hours of research and then there are the questions that make us ponder, and the answers that get us into trouble.

I've always enjoyed the adorable joke about little Johnny who comes home and asks his parents "Where did I come from?" After much equivocating, and stumbling all over each other, his parents launch into a rather detailed explanation of the birds and the bees, explaining sex education in a manner that leaves little Johnny wide-eyed and terribly confused about it all. Then Johnny gathers his wits and replies rather nonchalantly, "That's funny! Jimmy says he came from Ohio!"

See what I mean? Children are innately curious about life. They are exploring and discovering every day. It is a blessing and sometimes a challenge when they ask questions we don't have answers to, but we must encourage them to keep on asking! How else will their world grow and take on meaning?

Believe me when I say, that as they grow up, the questions definitely get tougher. Questions about life, love and God surfaced when the environment was right and we had laid the framework for discourse early on. It was an amazing privilege to sit with our teens and ponder these points of interest. It was an honor when they came to us with a broken heart or a troubled mind. "Can I ask you something?" These five simple words opened the door to treasured communication that may not have solved the world's problems and may not have been earth-shattering in the big picture, but nevertheless, meant the world to us and our sons.

"Do worms have tonsils?" To this day, I do not know. What I do know is that it brought a smile to my face in the asking, for it meant their curiosity was piqued and their little brains were whirring and humming to figure out life.

"LETTING DOWN" IN PUBLIC

This is another one of those subjects that you never hear about unless you experience it for yourself and then suddenly, every mother you know who ever nursed has their own story to tell as well. Before I became pregnant and nursed our boys, I had never even heard the phrase "letting down" and if I had, I would have assumed it meant relaxing. So what's the big deal about relaxing in public? Don't people go out on the town to relax, have fun, forget about the stresses of work and family? What's the big deal?

In the world of nursing mothers, "letting down" certainly still means relaxing, but we're talking milk now. We're talking about that tingly feeling as your milk comes in and you prepare mentally and physically to nurse your little one. If you're not relaxed, that process can be difficult, if not totally stymied. So, letting down is a critical step for the nursing mom. In my case, it was an embarrassing step that occurred one day in public when I was very much in the public eye.

I used to sing with a group called *Sweet Adelines*. It's a women's barbershop group that sings four part harmony and I was the lead in a quartet. We had gotten a "gig" at a church summer strawberry festival and I had just given birth two months earlier to our middle son, Mark.

In typical barbershop style, we were dressed in white slacks and white blouses with red cotton vests and red bow ties to fit the occasion. It was a glorious, sunny summer day and we were excited to have been asked to perform. The weather was hot, bordering on sweltering even though the stage was shaded under a big tent. However, our spirits were high as we started off the first portion of our program and looked out at the smiling faces of the audience, happily gorging on strawberry shortcake.

The first half was well-received but during the second half, a baby in the audience suddenly began to cry. "So what?" you may ask yourself. However, any mother who has nursed her babies will begin to chuckle at this point in the story. You see, the sound of a crying baby can stimulate the "letting down" process in your nursing mother body, and before you know it, you are aching to nurse, no matter where you are. All I could picture at that point was the adorable face of my sweet baby boy!

I felt it but didn't realize that it was obvious to the audience. Some people began snickering and I noticed shoulders shaking as they tried to cover up their embarrassment and stifle their laughter. Then it dawned on me. I looked down and sure enough, the left side of my red vest was now soaked and had turned a deep maroon from the milk. We continued to sing as I turned the color of my vest and finished the program with a slight shrug. "The show must go on!" What a show it was.

PINK GORILLAS AND
THE FOUNTAIN OF YOUTH

We had friends who had two girls just about the same ages as our two older boys. We used to get together on a regular basis when our children were little. While the kids played and fought, the parents played cards and fought over brownies while we commiserated about the trials of being parents. We compared notes on such things as discipline, diet, health issues and school scenarios.

One of the things we noticed right away was the difference in raising little girls and little boys. Our friends had a giant stuffed gorilla, which their girls had affectionately named Lucille. The gorilla took up an entire corner of their small bedroom but was their favorite stuffed animal. You often hear of the importance of little girls learning how to be "mommies" from their own mothers. Feeding, changing and rocking Lucille was a daily routine in their household. This was no easy feat as Lucille was probably twice as big as the girls, who were both very petite.

One day we were at their home enjoying coffee and our weekly ration of feel-good desserts. (Did you realize "stressed" spelled backwards is "desserts")? All of a sudden, Lucille got dragged into the living room by one of our boys. Much to the horror of their daughters, our sons then engaged in a wrestling match with Lucille, who was manhandled on the living room rug as our boys began to jump on her and toss her to and fro in their make-believe competition. Our friends looked on in horror, as their daughters gasped, covered their eyes, cried and begged their parents for our boys to stop.

We ended the free-for-all by pulling our boys off Lucille and encouraging them to go find something less physical to entertain themselves. Our friends let out a sigh as the mom slowly said, "Well, I guess God knew what He was doing when He gave us girls!"

God always knows best. There are certainly things you will never experience if you have kids all the same sex. We tease our friends and say, "We never did pink! Never learned how…" So we don't know about ribbons and bows, dollies and baby carriages, dress-up or My Pretty Pony. Of course our friends who have only girls can't relate to model airplanes, GI Joes, Legos or Transformers. Clearly, they have had no experience with the Fountain of Youth on the changing table. There were times I wish I wore glasses. That's another tip they should give you when you take your baby boy home, but no…it is all a part of the whole experience that just wouldn't be complete if you had a warning ahead of time.

CREAMED HERRING,
GUN CLEANING SOLVENT
AND AN EASTER LILY

My frame was not hidden from You
when I was made in the secret place.
When I was woven together in the depths of the earth,
Your eyes saw my unformed body.
Psalm 139:15,16a

There was a board game on the market several years back called TriBond. The idea of the game was to figure out what the three things listed on a card had in common. For example: can't, won't, and don't. They're all contractions. Here's one that is a little harder. What do Buzz, Woody and Mr. Potato Head all have in common? If you saw the movies then you probably guessed that they are all characters from Toy Story. How about these three words: pride, troop and covey? This one's tricky. These three all refer to groups of animals: a pride of lions, a troop of monkeys and a covey of quail.

Well, here's my version of TriBond. What do creamed herring, gun cleaning solvent and an Easter lily have in common? You won't guess this one unless you experienced the same thing as I did when I was pregnant. All three of these smells made me sick to my stomach when I was expecting and didn't know it yet.

Wes and I had been trying very hard to get pregnant for four-and-a-half years. We had just about given up and were home visiting my parents for New Year's Eve in 1983. My parents had a tradition of having creamed herring on crackers as hors d'oeuvres to celebrate and although I don't care much for seafood, I love creamed herring.

Until that evening, I had had no symptoms of being pregnant, no nausea, nothing to give away the fact that I was finally expecting! Nevertheless, I took one whiff of that cracker and almost hurled. My parents looked at each other with surprise and then smirked as Wes and I said in synchrony, "What?"

When I became pregnant with Mark, I was equally in the dark. Again, there were no outward or inward symptoms that tipped me off to the pregnancy. However, Wes had gone hunting and upon return, decided to clean his shotgun. I remember it vividly. We were in our den, enjoying a TV program after Scott was in bed. Wes got out his supplies and started cleaning the barrel of his shotgun and I again felt the sudden severe nausea as the strong fumes wafted towards me. This time, we shot wide eyed looks at each other and off I went to the pharmacy to grab a pregnancy test. Sure enough…there was the positive sign, clear as a bell.

With Ben, things were dramatic! It was Palm Sunday 1991 and I had broken my leg at church (of all places). One of our church friends brought an Easter lily from the sanctuary as a get-well gift. Imagine her surprise and chagrin when I threw up instead of saying thank you. I didn't mean to be rude—but apparently, #3 was on the way!

A BROKEN ANKLE
AND HUMBLE PIE

We love, because God first loved us.
1 John 4:19

Let us think about each other and help each other
to show love and do good deeds.
Hebrews 10:24

There is nothing more unsettling than letting a virtual stranger do your dirty laundry. No matter how sweet, gentle and loving this person is- there's something very humbling about allowing someone else to do what you have always done and want to be able to do yourself but can't.

Meet Phyllis. She is one of the kindest, sweetest ladies in our church. Also a mother of three boys, she showed up on the scene after I had broken my ankle that fateful Palm Sunday in 1991. This dear woman knocked ever so gently and let herself in to our home. She found me in my full leg cast, on pain killers, tearful and helpless on our den couch, and announced to me that she was there to do what I couldn't. "Point me in the direction of your laundry hamper and your laundry room, and we'll have all this done in no time! I know how much laundry accumulates with boys!" The next thing I knew, she was bringing me dinners and cleaning my house. She was my own personal white tornado!

It is an awkward position to be in when you know you need assistance from someone. You feel like it is such a gift when that help is offered and you have no choice but to accept. However, it made me weep to admit my need.

The most humorous part of this memory for me was the morning Phyllis came over to invite our two boys out for breakfast. By then, she was almost a grandmother in our home and our boys adored her. Scott and Mark went happily off to Denny's with Phyllis and came back two hours later chatting happily as they came in the door, stomachs full of food and heads full of tales about what they ate, and who they met. Phyllis shook her head with her eyes wide and a smirk on her face. "I had forgotten how much little boys can pack away," she admitted. Then she started to list off the portions our two had consumed, looking nauseated in the retelling.

Phyllis so gently and lovingly appeared in our lives at such a crucial time that I wonder if she wasn't indeed an angel. She modeled for me the idea of paying it forward, and so, when I can, I take meals or show up on a doorstep to give a new mom a break and a chance to shower in peace. It's one of life's little blessings that doesn't take much but means so much!

I read a quote once that said, "You may be only one person in this world, but you may mean the world to one person." Phyllis meant the world to me in my hour of need. She will forever hold a very special place in my heart for her generous servant heart. May we all be a Phyllis to someone to serve them a slice of humble pie in their hour of need and love them for God.

ANOTHER DANGLY: GOD IS IN CONTROL

It is good to give thanks to the Lord,
and to sing praises to Your name, O Most High;
to declare Your loving kindness in the morning
and Your faithfulness every night
Psalm 92:1, 2

Nowadays, so many couples opt for knowing what sex their baby is so that they can prepare everything in the right colors. When its baby number one everyone says, "Oh, I don't care whether it's a boy or a girl as long as the baby is healthy." Would you not agree? Well, that's a good response, since you wouldn't want to put it back!

When the couple finds out they are pregnant again they often want to know. If they had a boy, and it's a girl, they will want to change the colors in the nursery and lobby for a new wardrobe for the little princess if a baby shower is in the offering. The reverse is true as well. If it's another baby of the same sex, they can take a breath and figure that they know the routine and they're all set with baby clothes.

Then there's pregnancy number three. In most cases, I'd say, if the first two were opposite sexes, then we're back to scenario #1. "I don't care whether it's a boy or girl, as long as the baby is healthy!" However, if one or the other child is proving to be a handful or worse-a terror, somewhere around age two, you can bet Mom and Dad will want another of the opposite sex. "Junior's a demon, I can't handle boys; I hope this one is another girl!"

Finally, there was my scenario of experience. I had two precious boys, only twenty-one months apart and was wishing — no fervently praying — for a girl (for a change). In we went to our OB-GYN for our monthly checkup to see how things were progressing and we found out that at this point the doctor could indeed tell us the sex of this baby. Did we want to know? Did it really matter? Every child is a gift from God and it wasn't likely I would turn it down, no matter the sex. So…did we need to know?

True, I had enough boy clothes to sink a ship and another boy would have meant a world of savings in hand-me-downs. On the other hand, my relationship with my Mom was very precious to me, and I wanted that in my own life. I truly wanted a daughter to share the joys and challenges of being female: to dress up and have tea parties with when she was little, to usher into puberty in her teenage years, to cry with over broken hearts, celebrate with over blossoming romance, shop with for a wedding gown and commiserate with about motherhood as Mom had done for me. My heart yearned for a daughter.

I confess that when we asked to know and the doctor admitted that he saw yet another "dangly" (as he put it) on the sonogram, I burst into tears. I had to let go of my desires and put the longing for a baby girl to rest, especially since my doctor warned me against having any more children. I always had wonderful pregnancies, but my deliveries were difficult and increasingly risky. This gift inside of me was another boy whom I would love, nurture and treasure as I did his older brothers. This was God's gift to us, and God always knows best. I love our three boys and they were all healthy and absolutely adorable, or a "door bell" as Scott asked around age two-and-a-half.

When it comes right down to it, you have to know that God is in control. Isn't it comforting to know that Father always knows best? Three C-sections, three danglies! Now I look forward to sweet relationships with three daughters-in-law. I fervently pray that someday God will bless me with granddaughters who will invite me over for tea parties and let me decorate their hair with pink ribbons! The first sentence I will teach them is, "If Mommy says no, ask Grandma." After all, spoiling is definitely in the Grandma contract.

THE VACATION FROM HELL

guess every family experiences one eventually. We called it the vacation from hell for good reasons. It was the summer of 1991 and I was pregnant with Ben at the time. We usually made a trip to Cape Cod sometime in July or August to see Wes' parents who lived in Orleans, right in the elbow of the peninsula. The boys always had a great time, enjoying the sun and sand on Nauset and Skaket Beaches, sailing with their dad in the Beetle Swan, clamming for quahogs and steamers with their buckets and rakes, or visiting the Chatham Fish Pier where the fishing boats brought their catches of lobster and cod to add to the unique aroma at the dock. We often ventured into Chatham to shop in the quaint shops along Main Street or visit the Chatham Light House and check out the change in the sand dunes resulting from the latest Nor'easter.

It usually took us many hours of preparation for the nine hour trip across the New York State Thruway and then the Massachusetts Turnpike. After several pit stops, and a trip over the Bourne Bridge, we would find ourselves on Route 6 and finally taking exit 12, arrive tired but excited to start our nine day vacation. We usually tried to make the trip all in one haul to maximize our time on the Cape and our right turn onto Brick Hill Road marked our arrival at our home away from home: Grandma and Grandpa's house on the Cape.

This particular summer however proved to be a little different! For starters, both boys came down with the chicken pox the day after we arrived. We rushed out for oatmeal bath. The heat and the chicken pox made the boys miserable and they were itchy from the get go. It was an interesting beginning to what proved to be a longer than usual vacation. We assumed the salt water would heal their pox sores and after most of our planned vacation time had flown by, they began to feel more like themselves, just as we were scheduled to return home.

Then the expectant couple faced the unexpected: premature labor. Our baby wasn't due for another three months; this was *not* good! After a couple of days in Cape Cod Hospital, and a couple of doses of Tributylene to stop my contractions, our new friend and OB-GYN in Hyannis sent us packing back to Buffalo with Mommy stretched out on the back seat of the van and Daddy memorizing the location of every ER on the Mass. Turnpike and NY State Thruway! We made it back home safely, with our third baby still intact. However, we will never forget our vacation from hell, which culminated in a gift from heaven on November 19 that year!

A BOOK, A BOWL,
A WOODEN SPOON
AND A TAPE DECK

Bedtime stories were always mandatory in our house. The boys begged for them and fought nightly over whose choice of book would be read. It was definitely a family affair. We would huddle all together onto one bed, under the covers if it was chilly and the boys would cuddle close smelling of talcum powder and baby shampoo. It was a special time that was just as important to Mommy and Daddy as it was to our three sons!

One of the most brilliant ideas I ever had as a mom was to make the bedtime storytelling a fun, unique experience. We decided it would be great to tape the story in Mommy's voice with the help of Scott and Mark in the process. We had found many storybooks on tape in our local library and always enjoyed the telling of the story with sound effects and different voices. So one day we decided to try to do it ourselves. We gathered a book, a metal kitchen mixing bowl, a wooden spoon and our tape deck and began to create our own "library" of books on tape. I figured if there was a time when I was busy making dinner or doing some other mommy chore, the boys could haul the tape deck out for themselves and listen to *us* read a book all together.

The idea was that Mommy would read the story, then the boys would take turns sounding the "cue" for the page turns (in our case, the sound of a wooden spoon "gently" hitting our metal mixing bowl). It wasn't quite as delicate as I had hoped it would be. I was thinking of a chime sound but it ended up being more of a metallic thunk.

In any case, everyone got into the act. I would read the page and then point my finger at whomever wielded the wooden spoon. He would hit the bowl, held up by the metal ring by the other brother and so it went. We laughed ourselves silly when the timing was off, it went awry and we needed to back up the tape and start that page over. Nevertheless, I'll never forget the shenanigans. I'm not even sure at this point how many books we ended up taping, but it was still a brilliant idea and a fun experience for all of us, if you ask me!

I ran across one tape the other day, dusted off the portable tape player and listened to my precious boys' high-pitched voices saying, "Now Mommy?" Tears streamed down my face as I longed for those days back again. Suddenly my house seemed very quiet. I went down to the kitchen and looked in our mixing bowl collection and there it was: all dented with the metal ring torn right off. Smiles & tears...thunk!

"Another story Mommy, please?"

LEFTOVERS FOR HUBBY

Two are better than one,
because they have a good return for their work;
If one falls down, his friend can help him up.
But pity the man who falls and has no one to help him up!
Also, if two lie down together, they will keep warm.
But how can one keep warm alone?
Ecclesiastes 4:9-11

Count it all joy when you fall into various trials,
knowing that testing of your faith produces patience.
James 1:2,3

One of the dangers of having children is that there are only so many hours in a day and only so much energy in a person. When we become moms, our emotional and physical energy are being sapped by our helpless babe who depends on us for its very existence. God gave us that mother instinct to give every ounce of our being for their well-being. The problem is: at the end of the day, there is often not much left, if anything. Multiply that times two and then three and that adds up to trouble — with a capital "T"!

Wes and I often admit to other couples the fact that we had three boys and we ended up in marriage counseling three times. By the time the boys were settled down for the night, I had nothing left for Wes. As a nursing mom, I was often running on empty with many broken or sleepless nights in a row and when I finally hit the pillow at the end of the day, the *only* thing I had on my mind was sleep! In all honesty, that didn't go over really well with my poor husband who also wanted some of me. (Not tonight honey, I have a hegg-ache.)

Leftovers are never appetizing, especially if they need to be reheated. When what's left over is minimal, and we're still left feeling hungry, it's no picnic. We were smart to seek counselors who assured us that this was typical in marriages dealing with parenthood. Moreover, they congratulated us for addressing the issue and getting help. How many of us leave things unchecked, hoping the difficulties will iron themselves out, only to find a bigger mess down the road? We've always said that a marriage is like a car; it is much easier to do maintenance and take care of the knocks and pings than wait until it totally breaks down. It's a lot less painful too!

So yeah — three boys, three counselors...

The truth was that we were indeed deeply in love. We just had to figure out how I could get through my day without giving everything I had to our boys. It is a fine line, because kids will take all they can get, and that's where Mommy-time comes in. It took me a while to understand that when I took time for me, I was happier and therefore, everyone else in our family was happier as well. I'm sure you've all heard the phrase, "When Momma ain't happy, t'ain't nobody happy!" Wes was glad to get me out of the house for some time alone or with friends, because he knew that when I returned I would be a better mom and a more loving wife. We're slow learners — it took three trips to the marriage counselor before the light went on. I guess he'd had enough no-thank-you helpings of leftovers...mea culpa!

MY LITTLE SPACEMAN

Have you ever walked into a place like Party City or just about any big department store around Halloween and looked at the children's costumes hanging on the racks? You're lucky if you get away with spending only $19.99! Normally, the cost of some of these getups is closer to forty bucks. What ever happened to creativity and ingenuity? When we were first married and our boys were little, we tried to be smart with our money because quite frankly, we didn't have a lot to burn. Consequently, Halloween usually meant scraping up ideas in the cupboards and drawers to dress our little trick-or-treaters in something creative yet practical. Especially when they were young, the chance of them fitting into the same outfit for more than one year was highly unlikely. Of course, if you have all boys, or all girls, then there's always the infamous and oh-so-loved hand-me-down which is *particularly* enjoyed by the third in line.

Nevertheless, we came up with some relatively fancy costumes on little to no notice. Don't you just love when they would come home from school on a Thursday and announce "tomorrow, we're s'posed to wear costumes to school and march around and show everybody what we're wearing"? "Okay, guys, let's kick into high gear and see what we can scrounge up and put together."

One year, we had loads of time and only one child to dress up, so out came the aluminum foil and a colander. We cut strips of foil and pinned them to a grey sweat suit. Then we "gift-wrapped" a shipping box with tin foil that was big enough to fit a six-year-old and cut holes for his head and arms. Finally we put a colander on Scott's head and tied it on under his chin with some silver pipe cleaners. It didn't stay on very well but it only had to survive a march down the school hallway for ten minutes.

Another year we went all out. I painted eight-year-old-sized "bones" on a white cotton bed sheet with glow-in-the-dark paint, cut them out and pinned them on to a black sweat suit. First I tackled the rib cage, sternum, and arm bones, then the clavicle, spine, pelvis, femurs, and lower leg bones. Finally, we painted Scott's face with white and black paint to look like a skull and had him wear black sneakers and black gloves. We still have that costume, and I think it went through all three boys…maybe it will even get some use from grandkids. It was a favorite; definitely a labor of love worth the hours of labor and very cool!

Then there was Mark — the most adorable zebra you ever saw. We bought a black and white striped shirt, had him wear black sweatpants, painted his face with black and white stripes and made him a headband with zebra-like ears. He won best costume in the second grade that year. Boo-ya!

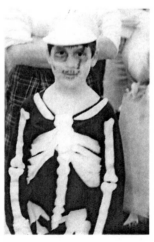

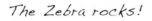

The Zebra rocks!

Are there any skeletons in your closet?

YOUR BOSS SAW
MY DIRTY UNDERWEAR

*"Cleaning your house while your children are still growing
is like shoveling the walk before it stops snowing."*
Phyllis Diller

There isn't a single mom that I've talked to who felt like she had her act together in the early stages of mommy-hood. We all go through years of feeling like we just can't get the laundry, the dusting, the dishes, or the vacuuming done. How often do we look around at the piles of toys and the piles of boys and wish we could keep even one room clean and organized for just one hour? I remember lamenting at the fact that people would show up at the door and I would graciously invite them in, all the while collecting toys as they overflowed from my arms, to make a path to walk safely down our front hall and into the kitchen.

I barely kept my head above water…maybe having enough clean clothes to put them in for school the next day, if I was lucky. If they ripped a hole in their sweatpants on Monday, a safety pin sufficed on Tuesday. Sewing? Who had time? Dusting? You could write dust me in the inches that accumulated on the bookshelves in our house. I counted on the family dog to lick our kitchen floor clean. It wasn't only the time to do these things that was lacking, it was the energy!

When my husband called and announced that his boss was in town and he had invited him for dinner, I had a coronary! The house was a mess, I hadn't shopped for anything special to make for dinner and I was still in my sweatsuit from that morning, un-showered and no makeup to boot. I did the best I could to straighten up and throw some chicken into the oven. When Joe showed up at the door, things were looking up. Dinner was almost ready, the kids were almost behaving and my husband was almost home.

Boss Joe asked if he could change out of his business clothes into something a little more casual and so I encouraged him to use our bedroom, the only room in the house where he could probably change without tripping over something and breaking his ankle. Big mistake! He came down to dinner with a smirk on his face and I asked him what he found humorous. He shrugged it off as my husband came through the door. After some shop talk and a few Cheez-Its (hors d'oeuvres — never heard of them) we sat down for dinner. I breathed a sigh of exhaustion and relief when Joe headed back to his hotel and the boys were settled down for the night.

Then I walked into our bedroom.

There in the middle of the room was a pair of my dirty underwear — shed unceremoniously that morning for a fresh pair. In addition, my bra was dangling from the closet doorknob like a lurid advertisement for Victoria's Secret. I was mortified! I haven't "entertained" a boss since.

FAKE TEETH AND
EYEBALL DIVOTS

used to have beautiful front teeth. Now they are both reconstructed with porcelain crowns.

When Scott was about six years old, we were coming in from running errands. I had just placed Mark down on the garage floor in his car seat to rummage around in my purse for the house keys when Scott noticed that his shoelace was untied. Having just started kindergarten, and being quite proud of his latest skill, he announced that he would tie his own sneaker to show me how it's done.

I watched as he wrapped one lace over and under the other, then made one bunny ear as he was taught, wrapped the other lace around it, pushed it through and pulled them both tightly. I was so proud of him and so tickled at the way he shared his new talent that I bent down to kiss the top of his head. Unfortunately, he came up at the same moment and my mouth hit his skull. He hardly felt it. I, on the other hand, started to ask if he was okay as I rubbed his head and found two-thirds of my front tooth on my tongue. When I realized what it was, I rushed into the house to look in the mirror. Oh…my… gosh! I looked like I belonged in the movie *Deliverance*! There, in the middle of my face, was a gaping, black hole when I lifted my upper lip to investigate!

Then there was the time I got a divot in my eyeball. Loving passionately and spending precious time with your children can be very, very dangerous!

I was sitting on one of the boys' beds, reading to them out of a Ranger Rick Magazine (cute stories about nature and environmental awareness featuring talking animals). We had just finished an article on forest fires when Scott grabbed the magazine and said flippantly, "I don't want to read this one anymore!" He tossed the magazine up over his shoulder and the page caught my eye.

There was a sharp pain and I ran to the bathroom mirror again to check the damage. Hanging from my eyeball was a strand of my cornea. Lovely. Fast forward to skip over the gross part and I admit that I had to wear an eye patch for two months as my cornea healed. Of course, my boys thought it was really cool that their mom looked like a pirate. If I had lost my tooth at about the same time, I could have costarred with Johnny Depp in Pirates of the Caribbean. I've heard that timing is everything…Darn!

The calm before the storm; another story time shot

REMAKING THE BED

Be patient, bearing with one another in love.
Ephesians 4:2

By wisdom, a house is built,
and through understanding it is established.
Proverbs 24:3

Have you ever asked one of your kids to do something and had their efforts not reach *your standards* by a long shot? I remember when the boys were little, one of my biggest pet peeves was their bed making. It was a chore that we thought each boy could handle at about five years old, at the start of kindergarten. Of course, in the beginning when they were first learning, it often looked like they hadn't done anything to the bed at all. Occasionally, we would walk in while they were in the process of making the bed to find them crawling on top of the covers, trying desperately to straighten out the bedspread with all their weight hampering their efforts.

Quite honestly, I had days when they were toddlers when I felt that all I did around the house was even less efficient and effective than their method of bed-making. As a mom, you can clean up one room, go warm up a cup of coffee in the microwave, return to the same room and find it in shambles five minutes later. It's the nature of the beast and really, what I needed to do was relax about it. Now that I'm an empty nester, I realize how futile it was to expect my house to be neat and clean when our boys were little. There was a bumper sticker I saw once that read: "A really clean house is the sign of a really sick mind." No worries there!

As they grew older, we still had to cajole and sometimes they were smart enough to ask why bother, since they would be climbing back into bed in another fifteen hours anyway. As juniors and seniors in high school, they just kept their bedroom door closed most of the time and we stayed out. There always seemed to be a method to their madness; it never ceased to amaze me how they could find anything in the mess, but they did. By then *we* were smart enough to pick our battles and the condition of their bedroom was not one usually worth picking.

Now I can walk around, glancing in each empty room and find the beds neat as pins for weeks on end. I long to find one rumpled, disheveled and slept-in bed, for it would indicate a long overdue visit from a son I miss and love dearly. After each went off to college, I would go into their room and tug on a corner of the bedspread, wishing them back for a weekend visit or a much anticipated holiday or vacation.

I have always loved the poem about the cobwebs that can wait, because until you have children, you don't realize how quickly the years fly by. We all need to spend time on the important things that matter because they grow up faster than you can believe.

One day Wes looked at me as I crept stealthily out of one of the boys' rooms and said, "You do realize that the message you're sending is that what they do isn't good enough?" Wham! I really hadn't thought of it that way. I could rationalize it any way I wanted to: I was only helping, they're too little to reach the edges, it is hard to get it smooth when the bed is against the wall, bunk beds are impossible to make…but I had to admit that what really bothered me was that it *wasn't* good enough by my standards. It wasn't smooth enough. The bedspread wasn't on straight.

The pillows weren't fluffed. The sheets weren't tucked under the mattress. You name it, I had an excuse.

Eventually I learned about the miracle of comforters. Not only are they comforting, but they hide a multitude of wrinkly horrors beneath their puffy layers. I was sure to buy comforters and a bottle of Febreze for each of our boys when they left our nest and descended upon their college dorms. In the long run, the appearance of a girlfriend always does wonders to clean up one's habitation habits. It's kind of like obsessing about potty training your child. I don't know of a single kid that's gone off to middle school in diapers, do you? As our standards relax on certain issues, so will our kids…and in turn, so will we. It's a beautiful thing.

I LOVE YOU THIS MUCH
AND EVEN MORE

Never tire of doing what is right.
2 Thessalonians 3:13

...set an example for the believers
in speech, in life, in love, in faith and in purity.
1 Timothy 4:12b

I t's so wonderful, and wise, to take notes from other parents who you admire. There is no better way to glean wisdom and insight into the ways of parenting than watching couples in action with their little ones. You take what you like and discard what you think won't work for you. You tweak what you've observed and absorbed for your own situation and pray for guidance from above. I couldn't get enough of learning from my pastor's wife, Sue. She was just ahead of me on the motherhood journey and so I watched and learned every chance I got. Creativity and a sense of humor were essential elements of her mothering.

Now, she is a grandmother and I see the same qualities, admiring her yet again in her brand new role.

One of the things that I feel is so important is lavishing love on your children in ways they will never forget. A youth pastor at our church tucks his daughters in every night, telling them "You are pretty, you are strong, you are talented and you are funny." When he gets it wrong or out of order, they correct him, so he knows they are listening for his sweet message each time. They know it word for word.

We told our boys "I love you this much and even more!" We would spread our arms out until they couldn't get any wider and then hug them fiercely and ask if they knew that for sure. There were often tickles mixed in and they would giggle and wiggle out of our arms. As they got older, the exchange grew shorter and we were careful never to do it in public. However, not a day went by that we didn't remind them of our love in words or deeds. We even went so far as to teach them the American Sign Language sign for "I love you" which is the pinky, index finger and thumb all stretched straight with the other two fingers of your hand curled into the palm. As late as high school, we would flash that sign to each of our boys as they climbed on the bus or headed away from us to join their soccer team. It was always discreet and always returned with a smile. Our married sons even flash it still as they drive away, headed back to their own homes.

I'm convinced that those kinds of reassurances built in them a confidence that would not be in place otherwise. Every child needs to hear those three golden words. Who doesn't? Somewhere I read a wonderful story of a parent who told their child that if every other child in the world was lined up in one long line that extended all the way around the whole earth, and that parent went up and down that line searching for just the right child to pick to make their family complete, they would be picked from the entire collection, again and again and again. What a beautiful message to grow up with as a son or daughter. What an incredible assurance of affection and love, to be told that and hold that in your heart as you grow up. Every child needs love!

I KNOW WHAT YOU DID

God blessed them and said to them,
"Be fertile, increase in number; fill the earth and subdue it."
Genesis 1:28a-c

Don't you just love when kids get to the age in middle school when sex education comes into their scheduled curriculum? You know when it happens! They start looking at you with a furrowed brow and you just get the innate sense that the tiny wheels are turning ever-so-slowly in that young head of theirs as they curl their lip and glare at you.

What ever happened to parents handling that sensitive topic? I guess not enough of us take our responsibility seriously, step up to the plate and address the changes, or the stresses and pressures of puberty. I remember my mom telling me of a school friend who menstruated for the first time in gym class and had an emotional meltdown because her mother had never had "the talk" with her and when she saw the blood she thought that she was dying. I can't imagine doing that to my child.

Now schools step up and take on the sensitivity of this intimate information. Not only are they able to teach things in sex education class that we, as parents, might wish our children never heard, but we found that the approaches often went against our values and the timing continued to creep up earlier and earlier. Abstinence, what's that? Safe sex, now that's the oxymoron of all oxymorons, isn't it? You may not get pregnant, but they don't tell you about the emotional scars it leaves.

The crux of the matter is — we can't leave for others the responsibility of ushering our kids into the facts of life session. The embarrassment (and we are all embarrassed to some degree) is much easier to handle in the company of the one or two people who brought them into this world, than a classroom full of peers. It provides a more respectable place in the barrage of educational material they receive if there is a breath of awe and wonder in the telling of it all. Rather than boiling it down to an animalistic act of self-fulfillment, what a glorious honor and privilege it is to bring God into the picture and explain that marriage is His design, and sex - His plan for two married people to come together as one.

Wes and I always appreciated the word picture of the tape on the arm signifying a sexual encounter with someone outside of marriage. No problem when it first goes on, painful when it comes off (or the relationship dies). Eventually, the tape gets less and less effective as it loses its stickiness. Moreover, as a young person experimenting with sex chooses many partners, eventually the beauty of what God intended to be the most intimate part of marriage loses its splendor.

When I was very pregnant with Ben, one of the young boys in our church walked up to me in the hallway. He was at that ripe age in middle school when sex education was just being introduced. He drew up one side of his mouth in a disgusted grimace and loudly

I know what YOU did!

announced, "I know what you did!" I daresay, I almost had the baby right there and then. It was all I could do to *not* respond, "Yeah, ugh, three times! Can you believe it?"

BOYS WILL BE BOYS

Those whom I love, I reprove and discipline.
Rev. 3:19

Folly is bound up in the heart of a child
but the rod of discipline will drive it far from him.
Proverbs 22:15

Remember my story in a previous chapter about the cousins and the cornmeal? You have to agree with me if you're a mom that you always have this eerie feeling when things just aren't right. One day as Scott and Mark played upstairs with their friend, my mommy sixth sense revved into high gear. I had heard the boys playing in one of the upstairs bedrooms and doing the typical amount of quarreling over Lego pieces and other toys as they spent the afternoon with their best buddy. All was normal.

I was down in the kitchen getting dinner started and keeping baby Ben happy and entertained in his nip-nap on the kitchen counter. It was summer and the weather was balmy and pleasant. I remember the front door being open with the screen door allowing the sounds of the traffic on our street to waft through the house. The evening was promising to be delightful. Maybe we'd get the neighborhood gang together for an impromptu game of soccer. There were six little boys all around the same age in various houses on our block who ended up growing up together in elementary school. They were like the Sandlot gang; always hanging at each other's homes, walking to school side by side, having sleepovers and Lego competitions, and playing in band together. They were inseparable.

Our older two were only about seven and five years old—just the right age to encourage that competitive nature that is so *male*. Their neighbor friend was Scott's age. Before long, the competition turned to who could hit the friend's house next door by peeing out the bedroom window? It had grown very quiet as the boys took turns positioning themselves against the windowsill to see who had the best equipment and the greatest capacity to reach across the narrow side yard.

Imagine my creeping up the carpeted hall stairs and stealthily inching my way toward their room to poke my head in quietly and find out what they were up to. It is always a parental challenge to discipline with firmness when what you really want to do is burst out laughing. I stated calmly that I thought perhaps there was something else they could find to do that did not involve messing up our friends' siding. However, when I returned to the kitchen I immediately called Wes to relay the story in hushed tones as I tried hard to squelch my guffaws.

The moral of this story: to pee or not to pee, that is the question!

THE DADDY TOLL BOOTH

Imitate God, since you are the children He loves.
Live in love as Christ also loved us.
Ephesians 5:1, 2

One of the biggest pleasures of being a mom was watching my husband being a dad. Every time he interacted with our boys in his loving, caring, fun, humorous, mischievous way, I fell more in love with him. In the beginning of our parenting, I fell in love again, watching him cradle our helpless newborns in his strong arms. With Scott, he was awkward at first, but it soon became second nature and he filled his daddy role with zest.

When our boys were still little enough to thrive on silliness, there was a game they often played, either before dinner or just after, that the boys begged for on a regular basis. Wes would place a chair in a narrow doorway that led from the hallway into the kitchen. From there, he would play the part of tollbooth collector. As the boys excitedly lined up in the doorway, Wes would give them each in turn a silly move and sound to imitate before they could pass through the doorway — their toll. They had to listen very carefully to imitate it accurately. If they were off by the slightest "tweet," "honk," pull on the ear lobe or pinch of the nose in just the right timing, the "tollbooth collector" would shake his head solemnly, repeat the sequence and encourage them to do it again. Of course, the older they got, the harder the signals and sounds.

Woe to the son who did not listen or was careless in his repetition of the sounds and motions for he got a playful swat on the behind as he was finally allowed to pass through. The boys would soon be belly laughing and falling on the floor as they scooted past the collector without their penalty. As time went on, their goal was to see what they could get away with in errors. I watched from the kitchen as I made dinner, or cleaned up and smiled ear to ear as I enjoyed watching all my boys having so much fun. There were times I was very tempted to join in, but in my heart I knew it was important for our boys to enjoy this special game with just Daddy. It was their time with him — to see a side of him that they loved.

Besides the always-popular horsey rides on the living room floor, there were also gymnastics which involved Daddy laying on the floor and holding the boys' shoulders as they balanced face-down on his lower legs, held on by his feet. He would count one-two-three and flip them over his body, supporting their shoulders upside down, to land past his head. It took me a while to be able to watch that one, but Wes always assured me they would be fine.

God knew what he was doing when he gave us boys! I had a husband who was the perfect father for boys. I heard said once: "If I had known how fun it would be to have grandkids, I would have had them first!" We're glad we didn't. It has been great practice for grandkids when they come.

Father-son bonding time

A tender moment for a
tender-hearted father.

A NO THANK YOU HELPING
AND CLEAN BREAD

She watches over the affairs of her household
and does not eat the bread of idleness.
Proverbs 31:27

Way back in the beginning when the boys were little and extremely picky about what they liked to eat, we instated what we called the "no-thank-you-helping." It was just what it sounded like: a very little taste of something that the boys were not really keen on having, that they were required just to try. So often, they would judge a food by how it looked or smelled and once they tasted it, they would find that it wasn't so bad after all — or better yet, that they really liked it! I'm not sure how often they would admit that, but nevertheless, a "no-thank-you-helping" went around the table on many occasions. More often than not, it was a no-thank-you-helping of vegetables. Consequently, if you asked our guys now, they would probably say that the foods they enjoy seriously outnumber the foods they do not like.

We often invited one of the boys' friends over to have supper with our family and they would frequently turn their noses up at things we offered for dinner on a regular basis. Many had never tried things like artichokes, pomegranates, chocolate chip pancakes with peanut butter, Brussels sprouts, venison, the list goes on and on. Our boys had no-thank-you-helpings of all of them. They don't like all of them, but they have tried them all.

Sometimes, the no-thank-you was just a misunderstanding. One afternoon when Scotty was still in pre-K, we invited one of his buddies over to play and stay for lunch. I remember his name was Michael. I don't remember a whole lot more about him other than this one visit. I don't think I will ever forget it!

I had gotten on a health kick right around that time and decided to buy whole wheat products for our family since it was advised as a healthier way to go. So, while the boys were playing, I prepared some peanut butter and jelly sandwiches on whole wheat bread with orange slices and a glass of milk for them. Cookies sufficed for a treat if they finished their lunches.

When I called them to the table, Michael took one look at his lunch, on the Barney the dinosaur plate in front of him, made a disgusted grimace and stated in a very put-off tone that his mother always gave him *clean* bread. After almost spewing my mouthful of coffee all over the kitchen counter, I gently explained to Michael that this was not *dirty* bread, just a different kind of bread called whole wheat. I regained my composure and offered to make him another sandwich on white bread. He took me up on my offer and both boys ate heartily.

I will never forget his face or the tone of his young voice. His face spoke louder than his words: "No thank you!"

I'M GOING TO KILL YOU

and Other Words You Can't Take Back

He who guards his mouth and his tongue
keeps himself from calamity.
Proverbs 21:23

Everyone should be quick to listen, slow to speak
and slow to become angry.
James 1:19

How often do we hear parents in Walmart yelling things like that at their children? Walmart seems to be a magnet for that: Light whippings in Aisle 4! I confess, one day I was one of those moms who had had all her buttons pushed and had one last nerve which finally frayed and snapped. I don't remember for sure what we were shopping for, but I do remember that the boys were whiney, getting into trouble and begging for this, that and everything. I finally lost it.

I grabbed Scott's arm and I spun him around as I gritted my teeth. "I'm going to kill you!" I hissed. Oh...my...gosh! You could have heard the proverbial pin drop. Children do not understand sarcasm, or exaggeration. They can only in their limited understanding take things literally. I knew the minute those words were out of my mouth that Scott had done just that. His eyes flew wide open, his complexion paled and he said in a quivering, terrified voice, "Will you really, Mommy?"

If only sentences were a palpable string of words that could be reeled back in and reassembled in more loving phrases, but they are not. Once spoken, they can build up or tear down, bolster confidence or devastate self-image, instill trust or crumble assurances. How often have we spoken words we regret with our whole being for months or years to come? The Bible is right when it warns in Proverbs 10:19 — *But he who holds his tongue is wise,* and in Proverbs 15:1 *A gentle answer turns away wrath, but a harsh word stirs up anger.*

In Gary Chapman's book *The Five Love Languages,* he claims that everyone receives love in one of five different love languages: physical touch, quality time, gifts, acts of service or words of affirmation. If any of those things are withheld from a person with that particular love language, then they do not feel loved. My love language is words of affirmation and how I can attest to that theory. When words of affirmation are withheld in my life, I feel totally unloved. Words of defamation pierce my heart.

One of the most valuable things we can do as parents is to discover our children's love languages and speak to them in their own individual dialect. It is amazing how we can have three sons, all raised under the same roof by the same two parents, all three be totally different in character and spirit. What's even more valuable is learning to be wise, as Proverbs tells us and holding our tongue; especially when children are young and don't understand the subtle nuances of speech and meaning. My children may not remember exactly what I said, but they will always remember how I made them feel. God, help me to speak love into their lives every chance I get, no matter how old they get!

I WANT TO CHANGE MY NAME

Time Out for Mommy

A good name is rather to be chosen than great riches.
Proverbs 22:1

There is an episode of Family Guy where little Stewie, the baby with the grown up voice is badgering Lois, his mom. He stands near her and pesters, "Mom, Mummy, Momma, Ma, Mommy, Mother, Mom-eee, Mum." Finally she responds with an exasperated "What?" and he chirps, "Hi" and runs away.

Have you ever wanted to change your name? Have you ever wanted to stand in the middle of the house and yell to yourself: "Okay young lady, that's it! You have a time out. Go to your room, and stay in there until I say you can come out. Don't try to get away with anything while you're in there either! You just stay put until I decide you're good and ready to come back out and face the day. Boys, you are not to visit me, or play with me or call me at all. Mommy has a time out!" Then you march yourself up to your bedroom, shut the door, fall on your bed and breathe a huge sigh of contentment.

I considered changing my name more than once. Suddenly, it *was* different. I was no longer "Ann" but instead; Scott's mom, Mark's mom and Ben's mom at random times when they started school. For the most part, I learned to cherish my new identity. I heard, "Oh! You're Mrs. Van De Water!" and it had a beautiful ring to it — the wedding ring I have treasured for over thirty years.

Let's face it: you don't always want to be known as "so-and-so's mother" or "Mrs. What's-her-name?" Sometimes you don't even want to be noticed or found, for that matter.

Many-a-mother has self-consciously sat on the toilet with a child on her lap because her baby found her in the middle of something urgent. Then there are the mothers who lock themselves in the bathroom for just a second alone only to come out to the blood curdling cries of their child who has fallen against the coffee table in their moment of absence. I wasn't cut out to be a super hero but I tried to fly off the coffee table with a towel on my shoulders and split my chin open as a child of four or five.

Truth be told, I have always preferred the playpen. Who says it was made for the kids to go in? Do they even make playpens anymore? I climbed in ours once and laid down, peeking out of one eye every so often to make sure the guys were behaving themselves and staying out of trouble. It was wonderful. They thought it was a riot!

I suppose if I had changed my name to something that was unpronounceable by young tongues, then I may have gotten some peace; but there's plenty of that now.

THE FARM IN PENNSYLVANIA

Who is wise and understanding among you?
Let him show it by his good life, by deeds done
in the humility that comes from wisdom.
James 3:13

W hen Scott and Mark were in elementary school and Ben was still a baby, we had a black Labrador retriever named Lady. She was a beautiful dog and as the family pet, was loved dearly and spoiled rotten. Her one frustrating habit was bolting whenever she got the chance and we often found ourselves patrolling the village streets, calling out her name and collaring her to get her back home. We loved her all the same. On one of her escapades, we believe Lady may have been hit by a car as she gallivanted around the neighborhood, smelling freedom with every canine inhalation! She never limped or whined but we did notice that she was very protective of her hindquarters after that.

One day we had a little guy from the neighborhood over to play. He rarely came over and wouldn't you know, that day he said he accidentally stepped on Lady's back end. The next thing I knew, he was stumbling into our house, holding his face where she had bitten him just below his left eye and cheek bone. He was a bloody mess and I was totally caught off guard. I kept my cool long enough to call his mom, take him home, and offer to pay the bill as she sped down the street to the emergency room. Then I fell apart. He ended up with stitches which are now a scar on this handsome young man's face. We were lucky; they were kind and understanding and didn't take legal action.

What a dilemma. We weren't sure what precipitated the accident, but knew that if Lady had bitten once, she could bite again. When she nipped at our good friends' daughter, we knew we didn't have a choice. Deciding to have Lady put to sleep was one of the hardest things we ever had to do. Lying about it to our boys, because they were so young and we didn't think they would understand, was the second hardest thing. At the time, we told them that Lady had to go live on a farm in Pennsylvania where she would get to run, play and have plenty of exercise and fresh air. They seemed okay with that until one fateful day.

Scott was in tenth grade at the time he relayed this story to us after school. He said he was walking down the hall to class when a student walking toward him told his buddy "like when my parents put our dog to sleep but told me that they sent him to live on a farm in Pennsylvania!" What were the chances? Scott couldn't believe his ears! He came home very distraught, realizing that our story could be a lie. It took some fancy footwork to get Scott to understand our reason for lying. We had to work hard to regain his trust. Would the truth have been better? We'll never know.

Mark and Scott with Lady who "went to live on a farm in Pennsylvania

THERE WAS A FOREST ON OUR LAWN AND NOW A FIREMAN IS IN OUR DEN

The Lord will watch over your coming and going
both now and forevermore.
Psalm 121:8

B ack when we lived in the village, Wes decided we needed to be energy efficient and wisely bought a wood stove. At the time, I thought it would be a great idea as well, though I didn't realize how much work it would take to keep a fire going all day and night to maintain the house at a reasonable temperature. Then the truckload of logs was dumped on our front lawn. They were full sized tree trunks which Wes and a friend cut with chainsaws and split with a wood splitter out on our driveway. We were most certainly the talk of the town at the time. It was quite the production to get a winter's worth of wood for the stove stacked into our garage.

Our wood stove stood snugly against the fireplace in our den and we taught the boys the word "HOT!" right away. We had a screen which kept them at a safe distance and we always kept an eye on them when they were playing in the den. They learned a healthy respect for the stove early on although Mark fell against the screen one morning and cut his face. He carries a faint scar to this day which you have to lean closely to see. We should have predicted trouble then.

One day, Wes was off on business and I had loaded the wood stove to keep the house warm. I don't remember if I left the vent open too wide or the door cracked open too long, but before I knew it, I heard the sound of a freight train roaring through our den. If you've never experienced a chimney fire, it's quite terrifying. I can tell you, it scared me to death!

I called the fire department and if we thought we were the talk of the neighborhood with the forest on our lawn, it was nothing compared to the firefighters in our den. They were at our door in minutes in their firefighting garb, hauling the fiery logs out of the stove onto asbestos mats on the den floor. I felt a little like ET must have felt in the movie when all the scientists were buzzing around him like flies in their hazmat suits. I remember our boys being terrified, huddled in the kitchen as nervous spectators while the firefighters did their jobs.

We were all fine in the end, but it took years for me to agree to having another wood stove when we moved from that home in the village and left the wood stove in that house. Just recently Wes persuaded me to get another wood stove. "They're safer," he promised, "and I pledge to be the one to take care of it." I relented.

The first day we got it up and running, Ben called from school needing a ride home. Wes had loaded it and you can probably guess what happened. Off he drove to pick up Ben. I was finishing up a piano lesson and before I knew it, all three of the smoke alarms in our house were going off at once! It was deafening! My young piano student started to freak out, a UPS deliveryman showed up at the door needing a signature and wondering what the chaos was all about and the phone began to ring. My next student came to the door and started yelling, "I know what to do! I know what to do!" as she jumped up and down excitedly. It was complete and total mayhem.

Did I really agree to this? Nonetheless, I must confess that there is nothing better than snuggling in a recliner with a great book and a steaming cup of mint tea in front of the fire-breathing monster, watching his flames lick the inside of the wood stove, begging to come out to play. I just have to make friends with it and let it know who is boss!

MARSHMALLOW WARS
The Soft Side of Healthy Aggression

Truly I say to you, unless you turn and become like children,
you will never enter the kingdom of Heaven.
Matthew 18:3

omething that we realized while raising boys is that no matter how hard you try to train them to be peace loving, they will still be aggressive to some degree. We had friends who swore they would never let their children play with toy guns, squirt guns or anything that resembled a weapon of any kind. Their children created their own, out of just about everything; by biting their sandwiches at lunchtime into the shape of a gun for example. We could relate!

We held to the theory that many things are good for you in moderation. How many stories have you heard of someone who was not permitted to watch TV or log on to the internet when they lived at home with their parents? Then they flunked out of college because they were finally out from under their parents' roof and that's all they did — spent hours in front of the TV or on the computer.

When our boys were little, we always insisted that they treated each other kindly but we occasionally allowed aggression as long as we were riding herd and it didn't turn nasty. A healthy wrestling match was enjoyed by all, especially when Daddy got into the mix. There's just something about the way boys are wired that calls for a tussle now and then.

The one battle that all three of our guys would probably tell you was the most memorable was our marshmallow war. We bought a big bag of marshmallows, divided them up amongst all five of us, and then went all out — pelting them at each other from doorways and landings in our circular floor plan. Our front hall connected to our living room, which connected to our dining room, which flowed into our kitchen and then into the den. Our home offered great nooks and crannies for hiding and attacking and no matter how hard you hurled the marshmallows, no one ever got hurt.

We did find out however that you have to keep track of them. Woe to the marshmallow that landed under a radiator in the winter time on the living room rug. Yuck! If you were lucky, you'd also find the "hairy" jelly bean from the previous Easter lurking nearby that never got found.

Silly you thought marshmallows were only good in s'mores! Granted, our boys pleaded, "Let's do that s'more!" Who needs graham crackers and chocolate? We found a recipe for good, healthy, harmless fun. Marshmallows anyone?

STRING BEAN BATTLES

The Art of Not Taking Yourself Too Seriously

"A good laugh is sunshine in a house."
William Makepeace Thackeray

know I'm not the only mom who ever temporarily found herself a single parent on a night when all her reserves were totally depleted and she could barely get dinner on the table. Having a husband in the medical sales business, there were plenty of nights when the boys were little that my sweetheart was tied up longer than expected or called into surgery later than usual and I was home alone to fend off the little nose-pickers and survive until bedtime. God bless those of you who single parent all the time. I don't know how you do it!

Then there were the business trips that took my husband far away — not often, thank goodness — and not really that far either! We have friends who have four children and the dad is often away in China on business. I respect that mom more than words can say for hanging in there and holding down the fort.

I had a different kind of single parenting experience dealing with a twenty-four-hour pager that could turn our lives upside down in the blink of an eye and the sound of a beep. I remember one weekend, being totally packed up to go camping as a family when Wes' beeper went off and he was called in to do emergency surgery. He often assisted in the OR when a pacemaker or defibrillator was implanted. "So much for the camping trip…Sorry guys! Everybody out, let's unpack the car." However, that's not my story.

This particular time, Wes was out of town on business and I was on my own with all three boys. We were having a very elegant dinner of macaroni 'n cheese out of a box and green beans out of a can. Does that sound familiar? I was exhausted and admittedly in a really bad mood. The boys had been grating on my nerves and I was ready to snap. No one was happy about dinner but I wasn't in the mood to hear the griping. After the boys had pushed all the right buttons, and just when I was ready to explode, Scott loaded his spoon with a green bean from his plate and grinned as he aimed it at me. "Don't even think about it," I growled as I squinted menacingly at my little troublemaker. His mischievous grin faded to a scowl and he lowered his spoon and his head.

"Get a hold of yourself, Ann!" I reprimanded myself silently. "Things aren't all that bad. He was just playing and he's awfully cute when he's up to no good." I realized that if anyone was going to break the bad mood in that kitchen, it had better be me. Well, I sneakily loaded a spoon with a green bean and let it fly! It hit Scott smack in the middle of his forehead and then — WAR broke out! That's all it took: 54 canned green beans, three mischievous whippersnappers, one happier mom and many relieved grins. We were finding green beans for months. Dad missed the fun…but heard all about it!

SUNDAES FOR
DINNER ON TUESDAY

O ur boys definitely thought we had lost our marbles! One Tuesday
night in the spring of 1996, Wes and I decided to really play with
their brains. Instead of making a typical meal of chicken, mashed
potatoes and peas with salad, or pork chops, rice and asparagus with
applesauce, we laid out a spread of sundae makings that would knock
their socks off.

Ice cream (four different flavors, all their favorites), hot fudge,
caramel and butterscotch toppings, chocolate sauce, walnuts, chocolate
chips, toffee bits, chocolate and multicolored sprinkles, whipped cream
and maraschino cherries were on the menu that evening. I guess we went
a little overboard because when we called the boys down for dinner and
they came barreling into the kitchen, they just about fainted.

All three looked at the table with incredulous faces, then at us as
if we had each grown a third eye and horns, then back at the table
again. Mark let out a whoop and dove right in. Ben bellied up to the
table and gingerly inspected the lay out while Scott just shook his
head and refused to touch a thing. It was so typical of each of the boys.
Mark was always our picky eater and if it was up to him, he would
have chosen ice cream sundaes every night of the week. Ben was our
inspector general who, as a rule, checked everything over twice before
putting anything into his mouth. Scott was a typical first born. If

things were not according to the rules, he wouldn't play and this was not definitely not following the rules.

While Mark and Ben inhaled their individually crafted sundaes, Scott insisted that we heat up some chicken and broccoli before he dove into his dessert. When he had finally had what he deigned to be an appropriate meal, then he would enjoy his dessert. God bless him! Now as an adult, he often eats on the fly at fast food restaurants, though his culinary skills rival mine when he has the time and inclination to cook up a fine feast.

We really tossed them a curve ball when we served the sundaes on that Tuesday, but it was something they'll probably never forget. We figure it's in the fine print: always keep your children on their toes by mixing things up a bit. When you keep them guessing, life is never boring.

My motto: Life is uncertain, eat dessert first!

A RINGSIDE SEAT AT THE VAN DE WATER RK BOXING MATCH

---

*"There is no greater agony
than bearing an untold story inside you!"*
Maya Angelou

*Love is not easily angered, it keeps no record of wrongs.
Love does not delight in evil, but rejoices with the truth.
Love always protects, always trusts, always hopes, always perseveres.*
1 Corinthians 13:6

There's just something about a bully that makes the hair on the back of my neck stand on end. It's not necessarily their size; you can have a bully half the size of their victim, but more often than not, it's the big guys who just want to throw their weight around. What I wouldn't have paid for a ringside seat!

All three of our boys were fairly small for their age until they hit the summer after their sophomore or junior year of high school. We have a photo of Scott from his sophomore year in marching band. He was planted between two seniors who were a good head and shoulders taller than he was. It was always a source of embarrassment until they hit that growth spurt and in Scott's case, put on a good six inches the summer before his senior year. When he returned to school in the fall, his peers were flabbergasted!

Before that wonderful, glorious summer of maturity however, he put up with a great deal of harassment from one particular bully. This individual will remain nameless (his initials were R.K.) and he got such a kick out of making Scott's life miserable. He would smack Scott's books out of his arms in the hall, slam his locker when he went by…the usual. It was when he held up a sign with derogatory remarks about Scott during a high school concert that we finally had had enough! We stepped in with Scott's permission.

We called the school, talked to the principal, ended up phoning this boy's father and asking that he talk to his son…nothing worked. R.K. continued to bully Scott every chance he got. It was a student's worst nightmare and one of our many parental heartaches. When your child is hurting, there is nothing that you won't do to fix the situation, and there are many things you can't and shouldn't do. We were beside ourselves.

One afternoon, Mark came home by himself on the bus. That was unusual, because when Scott was in eleventh grade, Mark was in ninth grade and they always rode the school bus home together unless they had informed me that morning that an after-school activity would delay their return home. When I asked Mark where Scott was, he responded, "He's taking care of business," like we were an Italian family with connections to the Mafia. I pressed him harder and found out that Scott had *called out* R.K. and they were meeting in a lot off school grounds to have it out. Luckily, Scott had thought to surround himself with some buddies, because R.K. certainly brought his entourage!

Interestingly enough, it took only a few good punches from Scott to the ribs and right between the eyes to finally end the bullying. Thankfully he never bothered Scott again. I think he was too humiliated that someone half his size could deck him. We never would have condoned a fistfight, and Scott knew that, but sometimes you just have to "take care of business"!

SPIDER WEBS AND
ALKA SELTZERS

Be happy, young man, while you are young
and let your heart give you joy in the days of your youth.
Ecclesiastes 11:9

One of the most challenging things to do as a mom is to come up with fun birthday parties for active little boys. I imagine it's really easy for little girls: dress up parties, tea parties, doll parties, teddy bear picnics, princess parties, ballerina cakes, gingerbread house making parties, make your own jewelry parties and gymnastics parties all went over big in my girlhood days. Put a gaggle of giggling girls in a room, say the word *princess* and you've got a party!

Now little boys are a bit different. When our guys were little there was "Chucky Cheese," a playroom of gaming machines, ball bins to jump in, tubes to crawl through...that sort of thing. Of course when they got older, we frequented Lasertron three times a year for a couple of years. (For those of you who don't know, it's a complex where they supply you with laser guns and you run around in the dark with black lights trying to shoot everyone's pack who is not wearing your fluorescent color.) Even as parents, we had a blast when our boys got old enough to invite a couple of buddies for pizza and Lasertron. We joined in the fun, embarrassed our sons, and everyone went home full, tired and happy.

When they were younger, it was more challenging to find something that kept their interest and sapped their energy enough to have them sit calmly for cake and ice cream later so they could get jazzed up again and sent back home to their parents! I was always searching for ideas and I have to say, two stick out as very memorable.

The first was a Spiderman party with all the appropriate "Spiderman" paraphernalia. Spiderman napkins, plates and cups for soda. Spider rings and "Spiderman" goodie bags with take home treats were on the list too. However, the "piece de resistance" was a spider web we created. We strung yarn above, under, through, around and over everything we could (chairs, pictures, tables, rugs, etc.) to create a web in our den. Each string started with a numbered tag and ended with a prize. The idea was that each boy got a number, found that end of his string and on the count of three, had to work his way along the string, winding it up as he went. He would deal carefully with obstructions and competitors as he untangled his particular piece of yarn to finally find his prize. It was quite a circus to watch as these six little guys climbed over and under each other and all the objects in the room to claim their rewards for their hard work. What fun!

The other unique, memorable party was a squirt gun challenge. It was one of Scott's summer birthdays, but Mark was an honorary member of Scott's gang and Ben joined in the fun as the youngest competitor. We cut holes for heads and arms out of black plastic garbage bags. They wore them like sacks to keep themselves somewhat dry. Each boy got a squirt gun and an Alka Seltzer tablet (drilled with a hole) hung around their neck on a string. The idea was to squirt the other guys and make their competitor's Alka Seltzer tablet disappear before their own did.

Then came the days when all they cared about was the food — and finally, the money! Nevertheless, whenever they're home for a birthday, even as grown up as they are now, there's one steady request: Funfetti cake! I figured out just today, that over the twenty-five years of birthdays, I've made about sixty-two Funfetti birthday cakes (give or take a few). To my surprise, Mark's wedding cake was made of Funfetti

— sweet memories! Ben still gets a Funfetti cake when he comes home from college for his birthday celebration! Who says you can't have your cake and eat it too?

"Stick' em up!"

THAT DIDN'T HURT

The Fine Line Between Discipline and Abuse

But also for this very reason, giving all diligence, add to your faith,
virtue, to virtue, knowledge, to knowledge, self-control,
to self-control, perseverance.
2 Peter 1:5, 6

And we pray this in order that you may live a life worthy of the Lord
and may please Him in every way; bearing fruit in every good work,
growing in the knowledge of God, being strengthened with all power,
according to His glorious might
so that you may have great endurance and patience...
Colossians 1:10, 11x,y

I f you got to know Ben now, you wouldn't be able to imagine him as anything but sweet, amusing, humble and charming! He has grown up to be a wonderful, sensitive and very humorous young man. However, when he was younger, it was a different story. He gave us fits!

Of all three of our boys, he was by far the most stubborn. Ben was so strong-willed that most discipline fell shy of making an impact on him. We adamantly believed in Proverbs 24:13 from the Bible that says: "He who spares the rod, hates his son, but he who loves him is careful to discipline him." Of course, the other version that is more well-known is: spare the rod, spoil the child! We believe that without fair discipline, children don't understand right from wrong; (fair being the operative word here). We never shied away from discipline because it was apparent to us that our boys needed to have very firm, precisely marked boundaries drawn early on. Truthfully, the blurrier the boundary, the more often they stepped over it. It never failed. How could we blame *them* if we weren't clear!

Another aspect of disciplining was saying I'm sorry as a parent when an apology was needed. I know what it is like to have had parents who did not model that for me as I was growing up and now as an adult, I have a hard time doing it. On the other hand, Wes is good at taking ownership of his part of a confrontation with our boys. Just because we are the parents, that doesn't mean that we never have to step up and admit our fault in the battle. We must! We're never too important to apologize and ask forgiveness. We believe our guys will benefit from that when they become parents.

Incidentally, it was our goal to never have them divide Mom and Dad on an issue either. If we let them do that, we were inevitably standing on shaky ground. So we did our best to make sure that the little ragamuffins never got a chance to "divide and conquer" especially when the ratio was three against two. We tried hard to make sure that we knew where the other parent stood on any given issue, and if we weren't sure, we would not weigh in with our opinion until we knew. How often did our kids go from one parent to the other, asking the same question, hoping that one would answer the way they wanted them to? Dad says no, you can't go to the party if no parents will be there, so let's see what mom says… Very dicey!

The years when Ben started to test the waters and push our buttons were very trying times for us. Yes, we spanked him when he was in elementary school — and he would grit his teeth, glare at us through tear-filled eyes and say, "That didn't hurt!" Ooh! There were so many times when we would have to take leave of the situation and get our bearings to prevent disciplining in anger. It took all our will power to not respond, "Oh yeah? Well, does this?" and spank him even harder. It is such a fine line between discipline and abuse. Unfortunately, our children can push us over that line if we don't control the situation. Ben almost did that on a number of occasions as he was stretching his little wings.

We're not sure what exactly flipped the switch. Maybe it was his involvement in youth group at our church, maybe it was his hormones that finally calmed down enough for him to see reason, maybe *we* relaxed a little and helped him understand that we were trying to see his side of the story. Whatever it was, he entered middle school a different kid. The real rip-roaring fights were fewer and farther between and we were grateful, especially since we walked away from those arguments emotionally spent, for they seemed to last an eternity.

Now, thankfully, we enjoy him more than ever, especially his sense of humor, intellectual conversations and his musical gifts as he finishes his high school years. We're sure the spankings didn't scar him for life and we know that those clear boundaries were an important part of our loving him. As parents, we never crossed over the line into abuse, but to be sure, it was a very, very fine line!

THAT HURT

The Trials of Being a Sports Mom

always pictured myself at my sons' sporting events cheering from the bleachers like any self-respecting mom. Having been a cheerleader in high school, I could whoop it up with the best of them, using my well-trained musician's diaphragm to project my congratulatory cheer for the tiniest accomplishment. Hand me pom poms and I am in the game! It didn't take much for me to let out a "woo-hoo!" that became my signature cheer from the stands.

My boys could tell my voice from the far end of the field, and even though they occasionally scolded me for embarrassing them, all three admitted that they appreciated our attendance at almost every game, despite our raucous spectator presence. It even got to the point where their friends would hear me and tune our boys' ears to my cheers.

When Mark was in third grade, he decided to give baseball a go. It only lasted one or two years, but we think he was glad he tried it. (Soccer eventually became his primary sport of choice.) Mark, like so many of his teammates, often got distracted on the baseball field by planes, birds overhead, or an occasional four leaf clover in the grass. It was challenging to stay focused when so much time would go by with no activity in the outfield.

One game in particular was extremely memorable. Mark had been entertaining us out behind third base by totally losing track of things as we quietly chuckled in the bleachers. Then it was his turn up at bat. Mark was a little guy back then and obviously new at the sport. The pitcher for the other team wound up and let the ball fly. Mark saw it coming straight for him and turned away to try to avoid being hit. Instead, the ball smacked him hard right in the middle of his back and down he went. You could have heard a pin drop as everyone held their breath. It took my husband's strong arm across my chest to keep me from bounding out of the bleachers and cradling my son in my arms.

Wes had the where-with-all to pin me down and let the coaches check on Mark as he lay crumpled on home base. He didn't get up for a while but he ended up being okay, with the wind knocked out of him and a big baseball sized welt and bruise in the middle of his back. I got a taste of being a sports mom.

That proved to be just warm-ups for when Scott hit high school and decided to try wrestling. I have a whole new respect for the moms who attend these matches, let me tell you. When you have to sit in the bleachers and watch someone twice your son's size pile drive his head into a mat, its brutal! Gratefully, I refrained from yelling, "Stop doing that to my baby!" because I would have been disowned as a mother, but it took all I had to keep my mouth shut. So much for being a self-respecting mom; I watched the majority of matches with hands over my eyes. This chapter should have been titled "Keeping Mom on the Bleachers."

For a mom who hates heights, the ultimate challenge was being a spectator at Ben's track and field competitions as he vaulted himself over 11.6 feet in the air to clear a bar between two standards (vertical posts that held the horizontal crossbar so far above our heads). I personally thought Ben was out of his mind. It was a technical and strategic synchronization of mind and body that combined to hurl him into the stratosphere using a fiberglass pole, and hopefully onto a mat, having cleared his goal.

I have become a stronger woman for having witnessed this insanity as a spectator. I am a stronger woman for having had three sons.

Our little athletes in action; gotta love those spectator sports!

Mark

Ben

Scott

Ben getting another belt at the dojo; a guy and his gi

Batter up! Mark takes a swing at baseball.

DEER HEARTS FOR
SCIENCE SMARTS

May our Lord Jesus Christ Himself and God our Father,
who loved us and by His grace gave us
eternal encouragement and good hope,
encourage your hearts and strengthen you
in every good deed and word.
2 Thessalonians 2:16

Our guys never passed up the opportunity to have Wes come to school for show and tell; mostly because their Dad had a really cool job and was willing to get right to the "heart" of the matter when he came in on Career Day to talk to the students about his job. Being a medical sales consultant in the cardiac field made him a sought-after show-and-tell dad, especially since he was also a hunter and always brought a deer heart with him for the science class. He graduated with a major in biology from Hobart College and his presentation was always attention grabbing and totally engaging.

Of course, there were the normal number of kids in the class who would gasp, turn away and sometimes throw up when Wes did his demonstration but overall, the students were enthralled. Wes would keep a deer heart from his hunting success in the fall and then freeze it for his presentation later in the year. (You wouldn't believe the kinds of things we had in our freezer over the years!)

After dissecting the heart and explaining the different chambers, arteries, veins and valves, he would pull out his demonstration pacemakers and leads to help the students understand how the job he did could assist cardiac surgeons in saving lives. It was such a source of pride for his boys.

The classes had their fair share of doctors, lawyers, firefighters, accountants, vets, bankers, and other business people from the community, but as far as we know, Wes was the only one with a heart! A real heart. A hold-it-in-your-hand heart! A daddy heart too; it was a pleasure and a privilege for him to be involved in his boys' educations and just the fact that he cared enough to take the time meant the world to our sons. We know that for a fact. We are convinced that it's the parents who stay involved in their kids' lives and in their kids' educations that have children who are well-adjusted and excel in their studies. When we showed our guys that education was valuable and it was important to strive to do well in school, our children picked up on that.

So the next time you happen to have an extra heart laying around, take it in to science class and see how it pumps everybody up. Deer hearts for science smarts; you just can't beat it

Wes really has a
heart for education

THE LEGO PRINCE
AND HIS MOM

here was a time when Mark was in middle school when he couldn't get enough of Legos. He was about as creative as any kid could be when it came to building spaceships of all kinds. He had the mind of an architect and the heart of a musician. No matter what the kit was, Mark would build it according to the directions the very first time he opened the box, but then it was his imagination that took over to form the most amazing flying machines you ever saw. We often considered taking pictures or having Mark write directions for the completion of these spaceships because we were sure that the Lego company would pay millions to have his plans for their marketing department. (Then college would be paid for, yahoo!)

Mark was always proud of his creations and no two were ever alike. We ended up accumulating thousands of Lego pieces over the years. Some Christmases, boxes of Legos were the gifts that all three boys received from the family so it didn't take long to have quite a collection. They now sit in a big bin in our basement for our grandsons someday and we're sure to be the coolest grandparents in town!

In the days when getting on the floor was not a painful thing and getting up off the floor was feasible—I would find myself right in the middle of the Lego pile, building my own creation right next to my boy. It was how I chose to spend much of my Mommy time and I got darn good at making spaceships as well. I don't know that I would ever dare to compare, but I certainly could hold my own in the Lego spaceship building category.

When Mark was in high school, he latched on to the creative hobby of molding little critters out of clay that was baked to harden. These miniatures were amazing! They were colorful, mythical, whimsical creatures that each had their own individual personality and came complete with clay accessories like pets, miniature white clay snowballs, skis, mountain climbing gear, weapons, etc. They had long robes, long noses, sometimes googly eyes, horns or extra big ears and they were absolutely adorable. At that point we considered trying to market them to Burger King or McDonald's for their Happy Meals, but that plan never got off the ground either. They sit on a shelf in our den to this day, collecting dust but still bringing a smile. We did end up paying for Mark's college education, but the memories are priceless!

The Lego Prince
and his creations

HOCKEY SHOTS
BEFORE THE BUS STOPS

M y dear husband grew up in Western Massachusetts and was a hockey player from age four. He played as a little tyke all the way up through high school, when he managed to grab the title of All-Western Massachusetts defenseman, back in 1974. He looked at colleges with hockey teams but ended up at Hobart College where we met in 1976. God had a plan.

He continued to play hockey in college then joined a league once we were married and continued to play even after we started having children. Although our guys never grabbed hold of the hockey bug (which broke Wes' heart) they did gravitate towards soccer which all three played through their junior years of high school. Wes coached them all in turn, starting with Scott at the age of five and ending with Ben at the age of sixteen. We did the math! Eighteen years! That's plenty of coaching!

We had friends whose sons were involved with travel hockey leagues that drove hundreds of miles in the wee morning hours (even on Sundays) to get their boys to a game out of state. I was always secretly relieved that we were never into sports that deeply. Coaching, yes! That was an honor that Wes thoroughly enjoyed. It gave him one-on-one time (or rather, one-on-fifteen) with each of our boys and he was great at it; very patient, very encouraging, never obnoxious or ridiculing toward his players. His teams loved him and so did the parents. It was refreshing to hear all the positive comments compared to the boisterous criticism that sometimes came from the other side of the field. Many a parent thanked Wes at the end of the season for his sportsmanship and role modeling.

Though our sons chose soccer teams over official ice hockey teams, they always enjoyed hockey with their Dad in the driveway. Often, on cold wintry mornings, Wes would get out there (more so with Ben than either of his older brothers) before the bus was due, and grab two hockey sticks and a puck. They would pass the puck back and forth, trying to out-shoot the other before the bus pulled up in front of our house.

I remember noticing a couple of faces plastered to the bus windows, watching the end of a hockey fest in the driveway. Was it jealousy and astonishment that I saw on those young faces? I just had to chuckle. How many Dads ever took the time to grab a short, friendly fun competition with their boy in the driveway on a frosty morning? It was a wonderful sight to behold.

Who won? Who cares! We all won!

MY MOTHER, MY MENTOR

When she was only 56 my mom was diagnosed with Alzheimer's and immediately became a student of the disease. She had been an English as a Second Language teacher and found herself giving the same tests again to her classes, never remembering that she had given them the day before. That experience and her fateful trip to the supermarket were the two tip offs that something was seriously wrong.

Mom had food shopped one afternoon and pushed the grocery cart out to her car. The fact that she may or may not have been able to find her car right away was no big deal. How often have I lost my car in the parking lot of my favorite supermarket? You go there so often. Did she wander, seemingly lost? I'm not sure.

On this particular day she loaded her groceries into the trunk and headed home. By the time she got to the house, Mom had totally forgotten that she had shopped. She probably settled into her after-school routine and made dinner with what was in the refrigerator, thinking that she needed some things and would have to make a list. She drove to school the next day and put in her normal eight hours, staying a little late no doubt to give extra help to some of her students. When she got out to her car, she thought she had better pick up some items she needed for dinner. Mom had no recollection whatsoever of her time at the supermarket the day before.

After filling her cart again with groceries, she walked out to the car and opened the trunk. There were all the groceries from the day before and Mom's heart must have leapt into her throat. How could she have forgotten so easily? She was devastated because she knew the signs immediately. Mom was no stranger to the disease. It had eaten away at her own mother's life and here she was, on the brink of the same diagnosis. I marvel to this day at her courage and perseverance in the face of such a debilitating illness that robs its victim of every last shred of dignity and confidence. It must have been terrifying for her to watch her basic life skills being slowly stripped from her grasp.

Mom had graduated top in her class in high school as well as college and had gone on to earn a Master's degree. She was an inspiring and life-changing ESL teacher, the first female trustee in our hometown, PTA president, a gifted musician, a devoted wife, and a loving mother. She was active in her church and community and impacted countless people in her short life. Most importantly, she loved her family and especially her children and grandchildren. In difficult times, she was the glue that kept our family together and was the one who valued relationships more than life itself.

At first, she was very high functioning, berating herself saying, "That darn Alzheimer's" anytime she forgot something or found herself at a loss for words. Over time, she lost all her basic skills. In the beginning, she sat in a wheelchair for hours—bewildered. In the end, we rolled her through the nursing home on a rolling reclining chair/bed. At first, mom began to have trouble putting full sentences together, eventually she was unable to speak at all. Over the last few years, she was unable to feed herself or take care of any daily necessities. We watched desperately as our beloved mom slipped away.

Her mind deteriorated slowly until there was no one behind those dark brown eyes and we mourned her passing over the twenty years that she suffered from the disease. It was a long and painful journey that ripped our family apart.

Consequently, as our boys hit their teenage years, there were no more phone calls saying, "Mom, I need your advice." There were no more chances to glean from a loving mom the fine points of mothering and the wise counsel of someone who cared about and understood the fragility of family relationships. How I longed to hear her voice on the phone reminding me just again, "There is justice! History repeats itself!"

No doubt she is smiling down from heaven as each of her grandchildren accomplishes something new and wonderful, overcomes an obstacle, ties the knot with their chosen beloved, or welcomes a new little one into the world that would be her great-grandchild. I can picture her rejoicing with each proud moment, lamenting every falling tear, comforting us all from afar. Her spirit lives on through the generations in each little kindness, every caring word, a courtesy given, and a hand extended in warm welcome.

God promises that in heaven there will be no more tears and I cling to that. I imagine mom, radiant and beautiful, happy and free of the chains of Alzheimer's, still teaching me how to live and to love my family—reminding me that being a mom is a privilege and was one of the things she did best. Loving her family was her gift and legacy to us.

My mom, Pauline

I WANNA BE LIKE MY DADDY

"Children miss nothing in sizing up their parents.
If you are only half convinced of your beliefs,
they will quickly discern that fact."
Dr. James Dobson

In everything set them an example by doing what is good.
Titus 2:7a

W e all thought when we were younger that we could get away with doing something naughty because we thought no one was watching. Sometimes maybe you did get away with using bad language, making a bad decision, or even checking your morals or ethics at the door before entering a given situation. Nobody mentioned your bad behavior and so, it got easier to do it again. When you think nobody is noticing, what difference does it make, right?

Let me tell you — when we have children of our own, that all changes. Or at least, it should change, if things we've said and done have slipped into the shameful category. Suddenly we are being observed every second of every minute of the day and don't think it's not happening. Children are like little sponges. We parents curse and ironically, we're shocked to hear a four letter word come out of Junior's mouth all of a sudden. "Where did he learn *that*!" we ask ourselves and abruptly remember our faux pas from the day before.

I read a very humorous section of a book once that told of a father who inadvertently cursed in front of his toddler when he stubbed his toe on an out-of-place kitchen chair. For the next ten minutes he tried valiantly to stop his child from using the same profanity. Then his wife came down into the kitchen and the child stopped talking as he was distracted by his mommy's appearance. When she stubbed her toe on the same chair, out came the same bad word, which triggered the toddler to start his chanting again. The father grabbed the opportunity and said to the mother "Now look what you did!" making her think that she was responsible for their child's expanding vocabulary.

As we learned, they don't miss a beat! We went to an amusement park one sunny summer day and stood in line for our admission tickets. I don't remember how old our guys were, but the cashier in the ticket booth mistook our two older sons to be younger than they were and charged us a lower price. Wes quickly pointed out that they were indeed older than they looked. She waved us away and said with a wink, "Don't worry about it!" However, Wes insisted on paying the right amount. The woman responded, "No one will know," at which point Wes replied, "our sons know how old they are. They will know that we didn't pay the right entrance fee." It was a quick interchange, but it was a lesson they will never forget. They were taking notes.

When we are parents, we don't get away with bad behavior!

I wanna be like my daddy!

Ben and Wes fishing
on our pond

" I caught one
too Daddy!"

I'M COLD SO
PUT ON A COAT

*"A sweater is a garment worn by a child
when his mother feels chilly."*
Barbara Johnson

I guess when our children are very little it only makes sense. In fact, we are told as new mothers that we should always dress our infant warmly in their first few months of life because their body mass is so much less than adults and they get cold much more quickly than their parents. Being as little and helpless as they are, it is the parents' responsibility to determine what is the most appropriate outer apparel to dress their babies in on any given day. Of course, that doesn't mean wrapping them in a fleece blanket once they're in a snowsuit on a blistering summer day for an outing in the stroller. Our infants have no voice of their own in that regard; no way to vote on what their comfort level would be. Don't misunderstand — they do indeed have a voice. I've heard it. Little ones cocooned like mummies in blankets galore, hollering to be set free in the middle of August.

As our boys got older, they developed a voice of their own and what is more important, an opinion. I guess Scott and Ben took after their father, while Mark, who was slighter in build, took after me. His brothers always wore significantly less winter-wear than Mark did. He would, in my opinion, appropriately don the hats, gloves and scarves, that his father and brothers would dismiss, to stay warm and cozy in Buffalo's sometimes brutal winters. However, their father spent the majority of our twenty-eight years here in Western New York in just a sweatshirt and scarf, occasionally pulling out the windbreaker to snow blow the driveway. People always looked at him like he was a half bubble off plumb! Scott and Ben likewise, put on the minimum to board the school bus and since they saw their father in sparse winter outer wear, I really couldn't fault them for their decision making. Ironically, Wes was always healthier than all the rest of us combined when it came to fending off winter colds and sniffles.

My favorite phrase, when they were young was: "I'm cold, so put on a coat." Most of the time, as elementary students, they cooperated and appeased me by digging out the thermo-insulated-weather-proof-northern-goose-down ski jackets and plopping a knit cap on their heads. Our winter woolies box was full to overflowing with all the outerwear I had purchased over the years, thinking they needed more to stay warm and healthy and that perhaps it was the color or style that they refused.

If I had had my way, they would have carried a portable wood stove with them in their travels or strapped space heaters on their backs. For all I knew, both their caps and jackets ended up in their backpacks the minute the school bus pulled away from our street. Now that I think about it, I'll bet they hurriedly put their coats and hats on just as they were knocking on the front door to be let in after school! They thought they had me fooled. Of course, *I* never put on a knit cap; hat head was a fashion faux pas I was unwilling to commit.

For at least two years, I have been in full swing with menopause and I am just now beginning to appreciate the other side of the coin. I am no longer the one shivering under the blankets in the dead of winter despite the socks on my feet, thermal underwear and a full-length flannel nightgown. Quite honestly, it is a miracle we ever conceived in December, October or March! I don't know how my husband found me under all the paraphernalia I wore to bed in those cold winter months in Buffalo.

Wes was always gracious as I nuzzled close to him and placed my ice cold feet against his toasty body.

Interestingly, I am no longer piling on the sweaters, coats, hats, gloves and scarves to go out to the mailbox or make dinner. Now my personal summers have me dressed in multiple layers that eventually get peeled away like onionskins. I start the night in socks and a button down sweatshirt over my flannel pajamas, which usually get discarded within half an hour of climbing under the sheets. Then I spend the rest of the night flinging off the covers of our bed. I try to resist the powerful urge to dissipate the power surge under the blankets by turning on the portable fan aimed at my side of our queen-size mattress. I fling off the blankets panting one minute, then grab hold and tuck the sheets and blankets back around me when my tropical vacation has given way to the reality of winter chill. What my poor hubby puts up with!

I don't doubt that the people sitting behind me in church on any given Sunday are totally distracted by the putting on and taking off of all my layers as I quietly suffer through the hot flashes. Perhaps they are behind me taking bets to see how much I am willing to shed without causing a scene. I'm a hot momma turning heads again as I glisten in the middle of winter in sleeveless tank tops, taking off my sweaters as my cheeks turn bright red. None of my boys get it; they can't relate to the joys of menopause. However, as I furiously fan myself with the church bulletin on a frigid January Sunday and look around at the other women my age, I eventually meet the gaze of another girlfriend who nods knowingly and grimaces as she removes her jacket and does the same.

My new mantra these days is: I'm hot — strip! My husband thinks he's died and gone to heaven! Now in the dead of winter, when I'm sweating, the family finally puts on their coats and other outerwear as I turn the fan on high or open a window!

MY FACE BEHIND THE SPONGE AND MY BUTT IN A SHOPPING CART

Each of you should look not only to your own interests,
but also to the interests of others.
Philippians 2:4

In Mark's photo album, there are two pictures which I wish weren't in there. Yes, I am a prideful mom who wishes that every photo that was ever taken of me showed me looking as beautiful, slender, youthful and enchanting as any sexy fashion model in a magazine, shedding pounds off my body and years off my face. Alas, it is not so. Especially on "bring your mom to Youth Group and see how much of a fool she can make of herself in public?" night.

Picture #1: I am standing behind a life-sized, painted plywood cutout of a rather buxom, fleshy woman in a red polka-dot dress minus a face. I've supplied that face, through a head-sized hole. My mug is in total scrunch-mode as a water soaked sponge is being thrown at it. Of course, Mark got three tries, so by the end of it — my hair was wet and limp and the makeup was all over my face. It wasn't pretty — but I was there and I did volunteer!

Picture #2: The idea of the relay was to have our teenage sons put mom in a shopping cart (thank goodness I fit) and wheel her through a maze of traffic cones without losing control of the shopping cart and dumping mom out on her head. The son with the best time won. We didn't. However, again, I agreed to participate despite the way I looked (wedged butt down in the shopping cart, unable to extricate myself when it was all over but the cheering).

The Mother/Son events always proved to be a hoot! Despite the humiliating photos that inevitably showed up later in the week, I was always glad I went. That's not because I necessarily relished the idea of looking ridiculous in public (although I've been known to gravitate towards that) but because it meant time with my boys — just me and them, and everyone else in Youth Group of course!

There were many occasions when the boys got *just* Dad (like camping in Algonquin for a solid week — but that's another story). However, I didn't get them to myself very often. By middle school, I guess, they only hung out with Mom because *I* carried the credit card and *they* needed a new pair of sneakers or jeans. Then they tolerated my hanging outside the fitting room door while they quickly and quietly tried on clothes. We rushed to pay and get home in my van before anyone from school recognized the kid shopping with his mother!

So, if you are ever asked to go to a Mother/Son event, don't turn it down. You too can end up looking like a very happy, drowned rat and who knows, maybe you'll win the "butt in the shopping cart" relay and get the rights to brag about it for years at church. What mom could ask for more?

Got to love the Youth Group
Relay with Mom

" Ready, Set, Go!"

" Nummy, nummy,
good boy!"

THEY'RE CALLED
CHORES FOR A REASON

Discipline your son and he will give you peace;
he will bring delight to your soul.
Proverbs 29:17

O kay, I have a confession to make. There is nothing that torques me out more than when my kid tells me he's bored. There are a million things to creatively think of doing, if you put your mind to it, but we got to a stage where our boys were constantly telling us that there was nothing to do! Never mind that we had cards, dominoes, roller blades, skateboards, sleds, bicycles, dart boards, a ping pong table, movies on VHS, paints, Play-doh, Construx, marbles, books and the oh-so-loved Legos. Still, they would come to us and complain, "I'm bored! There's nothing to do!"

Now, as a mom (who didn't have enough hours in the day to do all the things on her to-do-list, who always felt like she was playing catch-up from the day before, who went to bed with her head spinning—thinking of all the things she needed to do the next day), there was nothing quite so prickly as the statement, "I'm bored!" Whenever I heard it, the scene from the movie *The Exorcist* (where the possessed girl's head spins around) would come to mind. I would clench my teeth and try to stay calm, all the while checking off *my* list the possible chores I could just hand over to my cherub while I ate bonbons and watched soap operas. "Bored chores" I called them.

I finally got to the point when I would warn them: "If *you* can't think of something to do, *I* will think of something for you to do, and *I* don't think *you* will like what *I* come up with!" For the most part, that usually ended the complaining, because cleaning the bathroom, and specifically the toilet, was nobody's idea of a good time.

Webster's Dictionary defines the word chore as follows: a minor job, a routine household duty. Well, if you asked our guys, nothing that could be described as work was ever minor, or routine. Once the request was made, there was eye rolling, a good amount of huffing and obligatory puffing along with an occasional grunt and finally, the chore would be done. It took all of about five minutes. It was rarely back breaking, sweat causing, physical labor that had them stretched out in painful, muscle agony hours or days later. However, you would have thought so by the response we would inevitably get. Eventually, they would toss out the terms child labor or Child Protective Services as they grumbled.

They all had their routine household duties, like setting and clearing the table, taking out the garbage, feeding the pets, cleaning out the cats' litter boxes and taking care of their rooms, which included making the beds. For the most part, they did those without griping, but any added chores, such as raking leaves or shoveling snow, were met with resistance on a regular basis.

I think Milton Bradley and those other game manufacturers missed a bet when they came out with their board games. They should have called them *bored* games. They would have sold millions more to parents who didn't want to hear it ever again. Bored? Clean the bathroom!

WHAT PART OF "NO"
DON'T YOU UNDERSTAND?

The rod of correction imparts wisdom,
but a child left to himself disgraces his mother.
Proverbs 29:15

He who spares the rod hates his son,
but he who loves him is careful to discipline him.
Proverbs 13:24

The shame of it all is that 1) there are no classes on how to be a great parent and 2) you don't have to prove you are qualified to become a parent. What other job in this whole wide world accepts just about anyone; whether they want the job or not, whether they had good training and role modeling or not, no matter how old or young they are, what character reveals about them, or whether they are committed for the long haul or not?

There were days, and no one is excluded on this count, when it would have been a heck of a lot easier to just throw in the towel and walk. "They are not listening to me! I give up!" and there I go, out the door, washing my hands of any responsibility for how they turn out in my absence! It's terrifying enough to see so many parents who do just that!

The key is that we need to toe the line, stand at attention, as it were, and take note. Eventually, we need to take a good, hard look at how our actions and our decisions affect the next generation. We can't keep pretending that someone else is going to pick up the slack, or accept responsibility for what we haven't done or refuse to do, like disciplining our kids!

When our boys gave me "lip" as youngsters, I often came back with the question, "What part of 'no' don't you understand—the 'n' or the 'o'?" In other words, this is a no-brainer and there is no argument here. Were there times it would have been so much simpler to give up, cave in, or go back on something I firmly stated? You bet there were! Did I? You bet I did! Alas, I confess, I did. Unfortunately, the lines would then blur and the boundaries would get wishy-washy and I had no one to blame but myself!

So yes, there were times when I caved in. I blundered through, trying to do better at what my parents failed to do for me, gleaning from friends I respect and admire the finer points of this parenting thing. I did my best and prayed that God and our children would forgive the times I failed them. In the long run, we all have issues that need to get sorted out as we reach maturity and become parents ourselves. In the meantime, we pray!

I have a framed saying, written in calligraphy, which I gave to my mother and received back when she passed away. The author is unknown. It goes like this:

Now That I Am a Mother Too

It seems like only yesterday,
that I was very small,
and telling all my friends
I had the greatest mom of all.
We always played terrific games,

and sang the sweetest songs.
You always showed me lots of love,
and taught me right from wrong.
It doesn't seem so long ago,
when I was in my teens,
and we could never quite agree,
on school or boys or jeans.
But you were always there for me,
and I learned to depend
upon the fact that you remained
my true and treasured friend.
Through the years,
you've meant so much,
and now that I am grown,
and have a wonderful family
I can proudly call my own…
I remember all the things you've done,
and I hope that I can be,
the special kind of mother,
that you've always been to me!

———————————

It is so true: until you are a mother yourself, you just don't understand what it takes to be the best mom you can be; the time, effort, energy, commitment, blood, sweat and tears. It is a 24 / 7 / 365 / 18+ job. Do we get that? I'm not so sure. I was definitely naïve when I became a mom for the first time. Aren't we all?

Another thought: I may be way off base here, but it seems to me that there will be a time in our lives when we can be a true and treasured friend to our kids. We strive for that and in many ways earn that relationship by the way we parent when they are younger. In my opinion however, that is not the relationship that we should have with them as they are growing and maturing.

Until they became adults, responsible for their own decisions, I always felt that I should be my sons' mother, not their friend. That could mean being pretty tough at times on certain issues and sticking to my guns when I said no! I've had friends who tried to be their children's best friend before they were out of high school, and I've seen the results of those questionable relationships. When the lines aren't clear between being a parent and being a friend, then discipline is never clear either. If we are so worried about being liked by our kids that we are afraid to discipline, the ramifications will be huge!

Our boys have all stated at different times, now that they are older, how much they appreciated the firmness we applied to the rules of the house. They realize, now that they are no longer under our roof, how much they needed those boundaries and guidelines. They are aware in their maturity how those lines, drawn boldly in their young lives, kept them from harm and showed them our concern for their welfare and ultimately, our love. Those firm boundaries also helped them learn how to make good decisions on their own as they grew.

I obviously don't want to be remembered as a "mean mother" but I hope my sons will remember me as a fair and loving one. *No* other mother loves her boys more. What part of "no" don't *you* understand?

THE FRONT OF THE BUS,
THE TOP OF THE CLASS

The wise in heart accept commands,
but a chattering fool comes to ruin.
The man of integrity walks securely,
but he who takes crooked paths will be found out.
Proverbs 10:8, 9

When we used to live in the village, we were literally right around the corner from the elementary school where our two older boys attended up through second and fourth grade. Our boys walked to school with four other boys and they affectionately named themselves the "Sherburn gang" (the name of our street). They walked like a wiggly, energized, expanding amoeba with twelve arms and legs as they turned the corner.

It was a ritual we loved watching. Michael, who lived farthest down the block would pick up our next-door neighbor, Kevin. Those two would stop at our door to pick up Scott and Mark, and then they would drop by Ryan and Jason's house, another two doors down. We have a picture of the six of them as little tykes gathered smiling on our front lawn when they were in about third grade. Nine years later we put them in the same order and snapped another photo when Scott graduated from high school. Four of the neighborhood guys were Scott's age — excluding Jason. Mark just tagged along for the fun of it and ended up an honorary member of the gang.

Then we moved. We needed a bigger house that would allow for medical product storage since that was Wes' business. The house on Sherburn was too small, with a dark, tiny office for Wes which barely allowed for any business administration to take place. So, we began looking and found a very unique house right on the border between two towns. It was an unusual situation because we paid town taxes for the new town, and school taxes for the previous town where the boys could still attend school. They were relieved to not have to switch school districts. They would see their buddies again once they got to the middle school and make new friends in the meantime as they finished elementary school.

Something that did change was the way they got to school. Now we lived where sidewalks didn't really exist, and near roads that were too dangerous to cross as elementary school students. Consequently, our boys had to adjust to taking the big yellow monster — the school bus! They did so through senior year of high school since we lived about three miles away

One of the things we insisted on right from the start, which was really a godsend, was the seats they chose on the bus. We had always heard that the troublemakers usually sat at the rear of the bus, getting away with their mischief as far away from the driver as possible. By sitting in the back, the shenanigans were often unobserved and so the "troublemakers" aimed for those seats every time. In the front of the bus, our guys found friends who weren't up to no-good, so as insignificant as it seemed, we believed it made a big difference in the crowd which eventually embraced our boys. It was the "nerds" who stayed up front, who eventually led the class in academics, musical talent, even sports prowess, and ended up admired and respected by their peers.

We never underestimated the impact that our boys' friends could have on their growing up years. So often, the crowd your kid hangs with determines their path. So many horror stories come down the pike that echo the sentiment, "My kid ended up in the wrong crowd!" Our guess was that particular crowd sat in the back of the school bus.

Do you know the song, *The Wheels on the Bus Go 'Round and 'Round?* I think they missed a bet — there should be two last verses. "The trouble on the bus starts in the back, in the back, in the back." Finally, "The good kids on the bus sit in the front, in the front, in the front — all through the town!"

The Sherburn Gang

A RACE AROUND THE
POND TO MAKE THE BUS

Love never stops being patient, never stops believing,
never stops hoping, never gives up.
1 Corinthians 13:7

've written before, how three boys raised under the same roof, by the same parents can still be as different from each other as night, day and well, afternoon. Our Scott was one of those kids who slept through the alarm clock on a regular basis. We never could tell if he heard it and turned it off in his sleep, or slept through until the poor thing gave up trying to wake him, or if he just decided not to turn the silly alarm on before he went to bed at night. Many mornings found us prodding, poking and threatening to pour ice water on him to get Scott groggily out of bed and showered. It wasn't an easy task. He apparently was allergic to mornings, like his mother.

Consequently, Scott became a pro at flying out of bed with about ten minutes to spare, throwing water on his hair, clothes on his back, books into his backpack, forgetting a healthy breakfast and making a mad dash for the red taillights of the school bus as it turned around the corner headed away from our stop. Occasionally he made it out there just in time. More often than not, however, he would stop flailing at the end of the driveway, noticing that the driver didn't so much as tap the brakes in response to his maniacal arm waving and frantic yelling.

Scott did know however, that the bus route took the driver down and around the block into a neighborhood behind ours where she collected the other students on her bus route, and then out onto the street behind us, on the other side of our pond. In any case, Scott knew that if he missed the bus at the front of the house, he could sprint to the back of the house, through our yard, around our pond, through our neighbor's back yard and catch it on the flip side on a street called Old Orchard. What a scene! It was rather humorous to see him, coat flapping, hand waving, back pack bouncing, as he bolted down his secret path, especially on winter mornings when the snow was knee high.

Mark sometimes missed the bus, but overall, he was fairly good at getting himself going. Ben was the star! He takes after his dad; up and at 'em without so much as a boo from us. Most mornings, we woke to the sound of him showering, getting ready for his early morning math, before school jazz ensemble rehearsal or whatever else took him into school most days before normal hours. It was very impressive.

I heard once of a child who was consistently late for school. His mom finally decided to wear pajamas and curlers in her hair to take her son in personally and sign him in late in the office. It was embarrassing enough to finally end the tardiness. Hmm, now that's a great parenting tip!

MOMMA BEAR AND
THE SHIFTY CHAPERONE

When Mark was in middle school, he sang with an amazing children's group named *The Western New York Children's Choir* which had a wonderful reputation of being very gifted and unique. Our region of New York (which, by the way, is nowhere near "The Big Apple") has always had a high regard for the arts, and music in Western New York is alive and well in the school systems and the theater district of Buffalo. Both NYSSMA (New York State School Music Association) and ECMEA (Erie County Music Educators Association) are organizations that promote musical excellence by offering students the opportunities to prepare and compete, vocally and instrumentally, as soloists or in ensembles. All three of our sons participated in these venues and are therefore all the more confident in front of people—whether they are performing, auditioning or interviewing.

The WNY Children's Choir was known for its excellent training of young voices as well as its repertoire of superb pieces for every concert that challenged the students musically. As audience members, we were never disappointed with the caliber of the performances we attended. The students had to audition and were selected from various school districts in the area. The conductors had inspiring and impressive credentials and made the experience enjoyable though demanding. This group was yet another example of God's divine plan for our sons. Scott was involved in the choir as well and they both had superior experiences that they would not have had elsewhere.

It was in eighth grade that Mark had the chance to travel to Scotland, Ireland and England with the group. They sang in various churches and schools as we traveled about and had a chance to sightsee along the way. What a fantastic opportunity! Of course, I say *we* because I immediately offered to go as a chaperone when I heard about the trip. A week with Mark traipsing around the British Isles was our idea of a great time! The one stipulation was that I would not be assigned to chaperone Mark and his group of guys. Consequently, I was given responsibility for a trio of young ladies who turned out to be very respectful and delightful. (They ended up calling me "Mom" - I had three daughters for a week!)

I don't know how the organizers of the tour picked their chaperones. We didn't have to fill out applications or mail in recommendations or anything of the sort. I didn't think about it at the time, but wondered later about the decision process by which volunteers were chosen, and here's why. As a parent, you would like to assume that when your child is in someone else's care, that person will indeed "care" for your child as you would. In my mind that always included as a top priority, unfailingly watching out for their safety and well-being!

Unfortunately, the woman assigned to be the chaperone of Mark's group of four boys was not quite up to the task. It didn't come to my attention until after the trip that Mrs. X (she will remain nameless and therefore out of the court system) actually abandoned our son's group in the middle of Dublin to enjoy a couple of hours in an Irish pub. Here were four young boys, oblivious to the dangers of Dublin's streets, left on their own to "hang out" and "meet back" three hours later at the park where she gave them her itinerary and trotted off. Can you imagine? If I had known about her actions that day, I would have hunted her down, hauled her out of that pub and…and…I don't know what! I guess it's good I didn't know about this until after the trip was over and we were safely home because *I* would've been the one in court! Call me Momma Bear!

TOO LITTLE TIME
TO JUST BE A KID

M aybe it is me, but I think we're heading down the wrong path with our children. Whatever happened to time for just being a kid?

One of the things I do to keep myself out of trouble is teach piano lessons. I've had as many as twenty piano students at a time, ranging from age seven to adults. It's something I've gotten better at over the years and now, I can't imagine not having that as part of my day. Here's an observation I have made along the way, as a provider of extracurricular education or an after-school activity.

It never ceases to amaze me when parents of my piano students inform me of the number of activities which their children are involved in. In many cases, their overcommitment either keeps them from practicing or prevents them from being able to reschedule a missed lesson. Admittedly, all the extracurricular opportunities are wonderful, but my question is, when do they just get to be children without something to prepare for and run to? Whatever happened to kickball in the street with the neighborhood gang?

I remember spending hours playing kickball in the street, "Murder in the Dark" or "Sardines" as a kid. "Sardines" by the way, is the reverse game of hide and seek where one person hides, and the others search for that player. When found, they hide together until they're all smashed like sardines in a can and the last person finds the pile!

Quite honestly, I think my parents allowed one music lesson and one other activity outside of school hours (for me it was cheerleading). With four of us, we were still busy as a family. The other day, a piano student's mom called and told me her daughter would have to postpone taking piano lessons for about a month because she needed to get extra help in Math after school on the day that she had piano lessons. Okay, I understand that Math is critical. Regardless, when I offered to slot her in elsewhere, the mother informed me that with her daughter's eight dance classes, she couldn't possibly fit a half hour piano lesson in anywhere else! *Eight* dance classes! What have we come to?

Were our kids spread too thin? We had to ask that quite often. Did everything end up half baked because there weren't enough hours in the day to do justice to it all? Could they ever focus on one thing they enjoyed and were good at, without watering it down to fit everything else into their schedule? What about homework? Did we allow them to run themselves ragged? It was often a juggling act and we were just as guilty as the next family of over-scheduling ourselves; not just our kids — all of us!

Speaking of running—what about the issue of exercise? I used to walk everywhere. You know how everyone jokes about parents who tell their children that they walked to school ten miles both ways, uphill, in the snow, barefoot? Well, I didn't go barefoot, and it wasn't uphill both ways but I did walk to school and everywhere else I wanted to go. I got my license my senior year, but never owned a car, so I walked.

Now parents are the ultimate personal chauffeurs. You just don't see kids walking anywhere anymore. Granted, it *is* a different world out there. Unfortunately, we need to be careful our children aren't walking *alone* anywhere in our dangerous world. Even small town USA can be turned upside down by an unexpected tragedy.

I have a piano mom who drops one daughter off for her lesson, goes to pick up another daughter from her sports practice, drops her off for her piano lesson at the same time she picks up daughter #1 to go to dance. Then she returns for daughter #2 before returning to the dance studio to pick up daughter #1. She has four girls and this is her Wednesday routine with just two of the four. God bless her!

I'm not pointing fingers, believe me! Our guys were very involved in many things: musicals, sports, youth group, private music lessons, jazz band, chamber singers, national honor society, "Good morning math" and on and on. I have to say though: if it ever got to the point where they couldn't handle their busy schedule, something got axed! However, *not* handling it manifested itself in many ways—the most obvious in stress levels.

Exposure is great; it is fantastic that our kids have all these opportunities and learn what they're good at and how they enjoy spending their time. Nevertheless, is it out of control? You've just got to wonder: what ever happened to kickball?

JUST WAIT UNTIL
THEY HIT HIGH SCHOOL

Do not be deceived; God cannot be mocked.
A man reaps what he sows.
The one who sows to please his sinful nature
from that nature will reap destruction;
the one who sows to please the Spirit,
from the Spirit will reap eternal life.
Let us not become weary in doing good,
for at the proper time we will reap a harvest if we do not give up.
Galatians 6:7-9

Our lives are filled with opportunities to decide how we will respond. We can choose to be positive and "look on the bright side" or we can always expect the worst and quite frankly, anticipate getting it! We occasionally heard people say, "Oh your kids are only in elementary school, it's worse when they hit middle school" or "Your kids go to middle school? Wait until they're in high school! It's brutal!" I'm of the mind that if you expect the worst, you *will* get it.

With our older two, we tried facing the high school years with open minds, not knowing quite what to expect. We didn't buy into the scare tactics of anticipating six years (and another four later with Ben) of tribulation. We would have our fair share of trials and miscommunications for sure, but we didn't project that it was going to be horrible. I guess we were looking forward to this new season in each of their lives as they approached their high school years, more out of curiosity than anything. We knew we had invested in them well. Thankfully, we had not spent their younger years ignoring them as we filled our time with our own interests. We had many happy memories stored away. Now we could focus on a new day and we expected to "reap the harvest" after doing our best to "sow to please the Spirit" for so many years. (Gal. 6:8)

What we got were ten fabulous years when the guys were developing their own personalities, learning to discourse about important topics, honing their senses of humor, practicing their communication skills, sharpening their people skills, deciding what kind of friends they wanted around them, and discovering their God-given gifts and talents. Quite honestly, we loved their high school years! They became their own persons. We began to see glimpses of who God intended them to be — how God was molding them into wonderful young men. It was an exciting time of adventure and discovery.

So take heart; expect the best. Don't buy into the scare tactics. Yes, our high schoolers presented new challenges in this new season — but we decided to love it. Those years may well surprise you too.

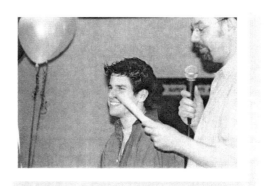

Heading off to leave his mark on the world, Mark at his Senior Youth Group Banquet

PLEASE DON'T WOO-HOO
AT MY CONCERT

You turned my wailing into dancing;
you removed my sackcloth and clothed me with joy,
that my heart may sing to you and not be silent.
Psalm 30:11, 12

B eing a singer, I have a voice that can really project with a diaphragm that makes it happen. It has been a source of pride for me for years at concerts, sporting events, across parking lots and in crowds. It has been a source of embarrassment for our boys at times. There is no mistaking Mom's woo-hoo! It is unique and admittedly, ear-piercing as I confessed in my chapter about being a sports mom.

It was when we got our new cell phones that could record events in video form that I noticed the volume of my woo-hoo. It was painful to hear the playback. My woo-hoos had previously been recorded on our old-fashioned 8 mm SONY video camera — but who ever watches all the hours of home movies after they are recorded? They sit in a box under the player and gather dust as the years roll by and the promises to watch them and reminisce turn to dust. Maybe when we are old and grey, and feeling very much alone in our empty nest, we will take the initiative and haul those movies out for a good cry.

At one point, Ben confessed to me that my woo-hoo was a little much. Well, yes, I confess that my woo-hoo is a little much. Yet as much as I tried to stifle the outburst when my sons did something worth cheering about, I could not. It came from deep within my mother-soul and it had to be let out of my system! I could not keep it in any easier than stopping a sneeze or a yawn. So, I pulled out my old excuse: "It is in the fine print on my mother contract that if at any time, I feel so inspired to woo-hoo, I can, as a mother, do so in good conscience, in support and admiration of my offspring's wonderful accomplishment, with or without their appreciation of said exuberance and expression of pride and pleasure!" So there!

When it came right down to it: they were always pleased. They certainly knew I was there and that I was paying attention. What child doesn't appreciate, down in their heart of hearts — that you have taken the time out of your busy day to attend their event and applaud their efforts?

However, I will always be incredibly envious of the ability my husband has for getting our boys' attentions. He can sound a "click" using suction as he pulls his tongue from the roof of his mouth — that you can hear anywhere. We use his talent constantly to alert our boys of our presence, have them find us in a crowded public place or let them know it is time to leave. It is amazing! We even found each other in a mob of people who were watching the Olympic torch as it was carried through Buffalo for the Summer Olympics in 1996.

YOUR MOTHER'S WEARING
A BANANA ON HER HEAD

There is a time for everything, and a season
for every activity under heaven;
…a time to be silent and a time to speak.
Ecclesiastes 3:1, 7b

Because Wes and I met through our mutual love of music, music has played a significant part in all of our lives from the inception of our family. Our boys grew up singing. When we went on road trips, we were singing and harmonizing a good part of the time. Playing instruments all together and singing as a family is a memory I will treasure forever. Furthermore, we roped our boys into performing for the Primetimers at our church (retirement age congregants) who were tickled pink to hear even Ben sing the theme song from *Winnie the Pooh* at the ripe age of about five. All three guys grew to be confident at performing in front of a crowd.

I suppose some of that experience was born out of two parents who were never too lofty to make fools of themselves in front of audiences. Wes and I enjoyed being involved in our church. Stand up comedy for our women's ministry was my thing. However, Wes and I also led worship musically for almost twenty years and performed dramas in the children's summer vacation bible schools over the years. I've never been really sure if this was a source of pride or traumatic embarrassment for our youngest, Ben. Scott and Mark were grown and out of the house by the time we were on a roll with that, lucky for them!

Understandably, Ben didn't always confess to being related to his two parents, especially during the summers in July when VBS (Vacation Bible School) was in full swing. The year we did a western themed VBS and had to come to church in cowboy and cowgirl costumes almost put poor Ben over the edge; not to mention rehearsing our lines day after day in cowboy drawl which drove him crazy. On our way to church, even after VBS was over, we would occasionally start speaking with our western drawls and he would groan, "OK guys, it's over, remember?" We'd pull them out again every now and then just to get his goat.

The one Sunday that the program was presented to the congregation was memorable. We pulled into the parking lot and Ben bolted from the car as quickly as he ever had, not wanting to walk into church with two people in cowboy boots, hats and denim with sequins. He was nowhere to be found once we made it in the doors. Poor guy!

I think the icing on the cake came when I played a Mexican señorita by the name of Sarita Rosita Juanita Conchita Anita Margarita, and I would always add—"but you can call me Rrrrrrrrita!" At one point, I pulled a real banana out of my hair (which was a long, black braided wig with various types of fruit and flowers in it a la Chiquita Banana ad), peeled it and ate the banana on stage. People came up to Ben after the program and pointed out the fact that I was wearing fruits and flowers on my head (as if he hadn't noticed). I know Ben thought, "That's it, my mother's gone bananas!"

NO ONE CAN
FILL YOUR SHOES
OR FIND THEM

...A time to embrace and a time to refrain,
A time to search and a time to give up,
A time to keep and a time to throw away,
...A time to be silent and a time to speak,
A time for war and a time for peace.
Ecclesiastes 3: 5b, 6, 7, 7b, 8b

Have you ever been afraid to walk into a room? No, I mean, really afraid! Like, you'll never find your way back out or something terrible will happen when you're in there? Welcome to the teen years. If there was any span of time for us to learn to pick our battles, the time was then because if we hadn't learned, we would definitely have been battling *constantly* over the years about the condition of our teenagers' rooms.

We're talking dirty underwear, gum wrappers, potato chip bags, muddy clothes, strewn homework assignments, unmade beds, notes from school friends, smelly soccer uniforms, mildewy rancid towels and wet bathing suits from PE swim class, hall passes for late arrival to class, grimy socks, you name it! If the World Health Organization ever had a chance to peek into our sons' rooms, our home may have well been condemned and torn down.

We often requested compliance with certain expectations—after all, who wants rats running around? The summer months were certainly easier to handle than the winter months when all the windows were tightly closed, allowing for absolutely no airflow when the bedroom door was closed as well. Eventually, it became a study in futility.

Unfortunately, the one big bedroom that housed all three of our guys at various times was directly within view of the piano where I taught my students each week over the years. It became a habit to mosey upstairs to our loft and gently close the door before my students rang the doorbell and I settled down to teach each afternoon. I could picture the horror on the faces of my younger students if they were to ever catch a glimpse into the chaos called "my space" by our boys. (Incidentally, as our sons got older, we made it clear: "my space" was still our space as long as they were living under our roof!)

In the first years of our experience with teenagers I would occasionally wander in and try to organize the mess; picking laundry off the floor to do a load which I knew needed doing or throwing out papers and miscellaneous junk that had accumulated and was obviously bound for the garbage can. I don't know where my sons got the habit, but they refused to throw out empty wrappers and envelopes.

After a while, I wearied of the ritual since the path I had so carefully picked across the carpet to the bed was soon obliterated and my efforts to make the room presentable or at least livable in my opinion were indiscernible. As I reflect back, it was always amazing to me that they seemed to know exactly where everything was, though often they would dig down several layers to come up with a single piece of paper or a matching sock. Their comment to my plea to make the bed was that it didn't make any sense to waste the energy. To be completely honest, I couldn't argue the point; I climb into bed every night with no one admiring my bed making talents except me!

BEN MEISTER

The Trouble with Nicknames

I will make your name great, and you will be a blessing.
Genesis 12:2

Have you ever heard a grown man called by a diminutive nickname like Benny-Boo; or how about Mikey or Timmy? Then there's Tiny or Beanie or Pinky! I don't know what it is about nicknames, but somehow it takes away the maturity and masculinity from guys at that critical age when they are trying so hard to be "all that" especially in the teen years of middle and high school and especially in front of their schoolmates. Pet names that were cute when they were toddlers or elementary age quickly lose their "cuteness" when they are among their peers and vying for a spot in the middle school pecking order. That age can be brutal and anything that can get grabbed as fodder for the mill turns into fair game for those seeking to play King of the Hill.

We never really continued the nickname thing after they hit middle school because "Scooter" and "Marky-Dano" (what Mark called himself when he was little and couldn't pronounce his middle name Daniel) were reserved for home and family use. These fell away with disuse and that was fine with both of our older boys. Ben never really got a nickname, because "Benjy" only reminded us of the scruffy little dog in the movie, and Benny was the name of our friends' golden retriever - so that one never stuck either. Occasionally, I called him Ben-Ben—don't know where that came from. However, "Ben-Meister" was my fallback when I was feeling especially affectionate towards Ben—as in, "Great job, Ben-Meister!" It was a nickname that went well with a slap on the back or a ruffling of his hair after an exciting soccer game with a goal or two. Normally, I reserved it for the car after he loaded his hazmat soccer bag into the back seat and plopped in all sweaty, muddy and hungry.

Unfortunately, I made the mistake one day of calling Ben by that nickname in front of the older, soccer teammates as they came off the field after a game. He was "low man on the totem pole," being a seventh grader, and the second it was out of my mouth, I regretted it. Ben's face first showed horror, then serious disgust. The worst part about it was hearing his buddies jeer and mock him all the way into the locker room.

It made Ben younger than his years, and took a good few weeks to wear off and dissipate as the soccer team moved on to more interesting targets. Regardless, I'll never forget his disgrace at my blunder and how terrible I felt at letting the nickname slip from my lips.

ALL I WANT IS LOVING YOU AND MUSIC, MUSIC, MUSIC

Finally, all of you live in harmony with one another.
1 Peter 3:8

T o be totally humble, they come by it honestly. Wes and I met through our mutual love of music. We were in college and involved in the same singing groups. I was the accompanist and he was the gorgeous, talented tenor in the men's glee club. Later, we both sang together in a mixed chorale. We had each taken music lessons growing up; me at the piano, Wes on the trombone. We both sang and played in various choral and instrumental groups all through high school and college.

It was in the genetic make up of our families. My parents were both musical: Mom played the piano and my father sang. Wes' mom was a wonderful soprano and his Dad enjoyed music of all styles and genres. The love of music was encouraged in both of our households and was woven into the fabric that made us who we are today.

So it was no surprise when all three of our guys started showing musical gifts in their talent mix. Even in the womb, all of them were subjected to piano lessons and undoubtedly heard Beethoven, Schumann,

Liszt, Debussy, Joplin, and countless others. Scott played the trombone and sang, Mark played the piano and guitar, and sang, and Ben played the trumpet, piano, guitar, sang and is now composing.

As the boys grew, our lives were filled with concerts and musicals. We enjoyed performances of *Robin Hood, Ducktails and Bobbysocks, Once On This Island, Tom Sawyer, H.M.S. Pinafore, The Music Man, Bye Bye Birdie, The Wizard of Oz, Godspell, Grease, Once Upon a Mattress, Pippin, Oklahoma, Beauty and the Beast and Little Shop of Horrors.* Incredibly, all three of our sons held leading roles and sang their hearts out while having the time of their lives. They loved the stage and entertained their audiences in lead roles which included Robin Hood, Tom Sawyer, Deadeye Dick, Winthrop, Danny Zucco, Prince Harry, The Leading Player, LeFeu and Mr. Mushnik. Furthermore, we burst with pride as their parents when the curtain went down and the lights came up!

To tell you the truth, the best part of it all were the friendships they made through their involvement in music, which kept them out of all kinds of untold trouble as they navigated through their teenage years. Yes, we were entertained, and delighted that our guys loved music as much as we did, and felt so fulfilled with that aspect of their lives. However, what we were the most grateful for was the sense of accomplishment and purpose that music gave them during years which could have proven tumultuous in so many ways. When there is no positive self-image, that's when the trouble can creep in. Didn't we all search for a sense of self-worth in those tenuous teenage years?

The takeaway: even if your little bird doesn't have the most beautiful voice in the woods, encourage them to sing or play an instrument. It has been proven that being involved musically in school opens pathways in the brain for all kinds of learning and joy. The friendships made can often last a lifetime; they have for our sons. Music brought harmony into our household because it gave our guys a fabulous sense of purpose and accomplishment. Don't we all want that?

Ben, a born entertainer

Ben as
Winthrop in
The Music Man

Ben as Ton-
Ton Julian in
Once on This
Island

Mark as
Prince Harry
in Once Upon a
Mattress

Scott as
the Prince of
Thieves in
Robin Hood

Scott as
Danny Zucco
in Grease

FULL CIRCLE IN
COLORADO SPRINGS

And we know that in all things God works
for the good of those who love Him,
who have been called according to His purpose.
Romans 8:28

Wes and I often marvel at how God works. You really can tune your life to watch for His hand in things that happen daily, although even when you don't notice, you can bet He's still at work. When Wes and I weren't really practicing our faith in the years just before Scott's birth, God still had a plan for us. His plan included a couple named Julie and Dave.

When I became pregnant with Scott, Dave and Julie were renting the house next to ours from an elderly couple who wintered in Florida. This young couple seemed very genuine and we hit it off well when we bumped into each other in the backyards. They had a little one-year-old toddler named James and being pregnant, I was very keen on watching Julie as she mothered her little boy. It was all very exciting to see how it was done. Julie and Dave were strong Christians and they wore their faith on their sleeves. During their year next door, they often invited us to go with them to church, but we always had an excuse. Truth be told, we liked sleeping in on the weekends and I guess I was rebelling in my own way against my parents and their strict churchgoing religion. We didn't know that what we needed was a relationship!

Spring was fast approaching and our new friends were informed that their landlords were returning from Florida. Dave was here in Buffalo on an engineering contract and the Buffalo winter had delayed production on the project he needed to complete. They were all set to move into a one-bedroom efficiency for the unknown amount of time it would take to finish the project. Could you imagine doing that with a one-year-old in tow? Not on our watch! We took a risk and invited them to move into our home for as long as it took Dave to complete his contract. God was at work and we cherished our time with them!

After they moved away from Buffalo, they leapfrogged all over the United States with different engineering projects and we thought we had lost track of one another.

Fast forward eighteen years: Scott decided in his junior year of high school to apply to the United States Air Force Academy. He had wanted to go there since eighth grade and he made it happen. Two congressional nominations later and he was visiting the USAF Academy campus with us to see what it was all about. We were blown away. It was beautiful. Scott knew that the military life and to a greater extent, *flying* was for him!

The last night of our visit, we were lounging in our hotel room. We had planned to drive up to Denver the next morning before flying out early on Sunday. I had some time to kill as my four boys wrestled on the hotel beds so I pulled out an old address book to update our contacts into a new one I had brought with me. When I got to the S's, who were listed there but Dave and Julie. You will never guess what the last address was that I had written down for them...Colorado Springs, home of the United States Air Force Academy.

I took a chance, held my breath and dialed the phone number, not knowing if it was out-of-date. When a woman's voice answered, I said tentatively, "Julie?" "Ann Van De Water!" she responded with warmth and surprise in her voice. The rest, as they say, is history.

We spent the whole next day with them instead of going to Denver. It was as if we had never lost each other. We talked nonstop, met their now-grown James who was himself attending college and his younger brother Jonathan. We felt like we had never lost touch; the old friendship falling naturally into place. When we left, Scott exclaimed, "I feel like I've known them my whole life." Did he know them from the womb?

The most remarkable part of the whole experience was that just before we left, Julie and Dave offered to "sponsor" Scott if he got into the Academy. He did indeed and they were there for him over those four years as his "home away from home" when he needed a break from the rigors of military training and academics. Dave took Scott boating, Julie had him over for dinners and picnics, and he hung out with their sons, relaxing off academy grounds. The blessing we had been to them in their hour of need in Buffalo reached full circle as they blessed us by caring for our eldest son so far from home in Colorado Springs. We knew that Scott was in wonderful, loving, Christian hands!

God is an awesome God. He cares about the smallest details of our lives. Even when we don't ask for favors, He supplies our needs. What goes around, comes around. We never expected, when we took Julie, Dave and their little guy into our hearts and home that they would be able to reciprocate so many years later by taking our big guy into their hearts and home. God always has a plan, even when we can't see His hand.

THE FOOD INSPECTOR GENERAL

Our mouths were filled with laughter, our tongues with songs of joy.
Psalm 126:2a

T o be quite honest, I always thought of it as a free dose of penicillin. I figured, as long as the whole loaf of bread wasn't green, we could pinch off the greenish spots and go ahead and enjoy the rest. The only thing that really kept me from enjoying old leftovers was the stench and, if present, the bubbles. We certainly had an abundance of refrigerator science experiments over the years. I often deliberated about reheating something that was questionable because I hated wasting food. Besides, Wes is kind of like Mikey from the LIFE cereal ad. "Give it to Mikey! He eats anything!"

That was until Ben got to the age when Home Economics was in his curriculum. They taught in middle school "home and careers" class that even one tiny speck of mold meant the whole item was bad. He began preparing food for himself because he no longer "trusted" us to not poison him with slightly suspicious food. Once he started making his own sandwiches for lunch, he became the "food inspector"! He checked everything with a proverbial magnifying glass to be sure there were no questionable spots. He refused cheese if there was a pinpoint of white on the end of the block. He threw out whole loaves of bread with pinhead sized mold. It got to be a serious problem in the summer.

Milk was another issue. If the container wasn't brand new — Ben would always check the expiration date, sniff it, then take a tiny sip. Any question, and he wouldn't have cereal that morning. It was especially humorous the day I made macaroni and cheese and didn't notice the little moths that had gotten into the Kraft box! I boiled the macaroni noodles and found little moth carcasses floating in the boiling water. I tried to get rid of them discreetly but he caught me! I've also accidentally cooked rice with moth larvae in it and opened flour canisters to find cobwebs. I don't even know what they are or how they get in there? I don't think my kitchen is unsanitary but maybe Child Protective Services would have a heyday if they inspected my cupboards, I don't know. I always considered myself a good cook but maybe I'm fooling myself—what's wrong with a little free protein anyway?

As our boys grew older, went to college and began shopping and cooking for themselves, they grew to appreciate all my supermarket trips and home-cooked meals over the years. We ate dinners around the kitchen table ninety percent of the time, believing that that was the time to see how everyone was doing. During college, our Mark was living in an all-guys' apartment his sophomore year and their refrigerator was normally empty except for beers and an occasional leftover of Chinese take-out. He came home, walked right past me into the kitchen and hugged the refrigerator, whispering "I've missed you!" Ah, a full fridge! It's a blessing you should never take for granted.

PASSING THE BATON

For the joy of the Lord is my strength.
Nehemiah 8:10

He gives power to the tired and worn out, and strength to the weak.
Isaiah 4:29

I t was just a part of our family life: the moment when everything was cleaned up after a meal, and we were hanging around, trying to decide how to spend our evening. The next thing you knew, there was a pile of boys in the middle of the living room rug, because one of them offered up a challenge and they were on! Before I could say, "Be careful that nobody gets hurt!" there were arms flailing, sweat flying, hands groping, tee-shirts ripping, grunts and groans sounding and flesh slapping against flesh. The joys of an eighty-percent male household! We had ourselves an honest-to-goodness world class wrestling match right here in Hamburg.

Of course, when they started getting really big, I was the typical wet blanket, the paranoid mom who was sure that it would get out of hand

and we would inevitably end up in the emergency room with missing teeth, a broken elbow or a ruptured spleen. Wes would dismiss my concerns, assuring me that boys will be boys and it was just as natural as fish swimming or pigs wallowing in mud. Give three boys an open space on a plush rug, and there's physical prowess to be proved.

It was interesting because whenever the challenge was put out on the table, Wes eventually got involved as well — either stepping in to help the underdog — (generally Ben, who was the youngest and until these last two years, the smallest) or defending his title as the biggest and toughest Van De Water in the house.

That was until Scott came home from his firstie (senior) year at the Air Force Academy. He was squadron commander, and had the leadership qualities that prevented him from expecting of the cadets under him what he couldn't deliver himself in physical stamina. By then, he was at his peak of physical conditioning, doing more pushups than I could count, and had unbelievable biceps.

It came down to a challenge to his Dad and before long, Wes knew that he was bested. As Wes tells the story, he realized Scott's strength and knew when to quit. He officially passed the baton to his son and acknowledged the strength that surpassed his own at this time in our oldest son's life. It was quite humbling to realize that Scott could arm wrestle his Dad and pin him in no time flat for the first time ever. So it goes…the baton gets passed to the next generation and a Dad looks on with pride as his sons mature and become young men of strength, stature and character.

That's not to say there are no more piles of sons on the living room rug though. Moreover, we look forward to the day when the pile is a group of grandsons egging on grandpa to join in!

LEAVING HIS MARK

When he was still a toddler, Mark had his way of coming downstairs on his belly, feet first. I don't think it was a unique strategy, as I've seen other toddlers maneuver in the same manner in other households. Mark would get down on all fours at the top of the stairs and then swing his feet around to slide lickety-split, face down, feet first on his tummy. (He and Scott were only twenty-one months apart so Scott was just over three when Mark started crawling and getting around on his own.)

One day, Scott was standing at the top of the stairs, telling me something about what he was doing with his life at the ripe age of almost four. Suddenly, Mark appeared beside him and in the blink of an eye, was pivoting on all fours, preparing to shoot down the flight of stairs. In the process, he swiped Scott's legs right out from under him.

I was down at the bottom of the stairs looking up when Scott's chubby little form hurtled through space toward me. I'm sure each mom reading this can relate to that feeling of suddenly going into slow motion. Your mouth forms an "n"—then an "o" as you drop what you have in your hands and reach out in slow motion to try to prevent the inevitable. With arms and legs flailing, Scott landed in a heap at my feet—my barely breaking his fall, it happened so fast. We've all had those moments as mothers, when time and space stand still and we watch helplessly as our children take spills or worse. I've learned that children are very resilient. He cried hard to be sure as I inspected every last inch of him. I let out a relieved breath and a prayer of thanks when I found no permanent damage. I'm sure Scott looked around cautiously before pausing at the top of the stairs after that.

Mark left no permanent mark that time, but he did "leave his mark" on the other side of the world! He enjoyed sports and was always up for a good-natured competition. In college, he loved playing Ultimate Frisbee—but as far as we know, he never left quite the same impression on Ithaca College as he did on Simon of Brisbane, Australia.

Our church's youth group had the wonderful opportunity of traveling to the "Land Down Under" to do mission work in the teen-suicide capital of the world. Our church had a working relationship with a pastor in Brisbane, Australia and sent several youth teams to minister to teens. They held youth rallies and spoke to their peers about their faith. It was a life-changing week for everyone, including our beloved American missionaries. Both Mark and Ben got to go at different times.

Of course, their experience included trying new foods like Vegemite, a dark brown Australian food paste made from yeast extract. Mark brought some home for us to taste and honestly, I found it to be very salty and kind of disgusting, but I hear it is very popular with most Aussies. Mark also learned about putting cucumbers on sandwiches, which we really didn't do very much here in the United States until Subway grabbed hold of the idea and included cucumbers on their smorgasbord of sub item selections!

When Mark came home, he admitted to us that during a game of rugby, he broke a kid's nose on the other team. Poor Simon will probably never forget Mark, for obvious reasons. I'm sure Simon looked around cautiously before standing in a scrum after that!

Leaving for Australia to leave his mark!

A TEARFUL FAREWELL

A man's steps are directed by the Lord.
Proverbs 20:24

He who pursues righteousness and love,
finds life, prosperity and honor.
Proverbs 21:21

I remember it like it was yesterday. Scott was off to basic training at the Air Force Academy and he had asked that rather than taking him all the way to Colorado Springs, we drop him off at the airport so that he could prepare himself mentally during his flight for what lay ahead. So that's just what we did. It was one of the hardest things I have ever had to do as a mom because I knew these next few weeks would be one of the hardest things he would ever have to do as a young man. He headed for the gate as I let my floodgates open and watched him disappear.

What truly lay ahead for him? Probably the toughest test of his young life: one that required not only physical stamina, but emotional hardiness, mental acuity, psychological strength; everything he had. The hardest part: we wouldn't be able to reach him except by snail mail during the three-month-long training. It was his hour to prove, not only to others, but to himself as well—just how much he could endure! It would show him that he had reserves far beyond what he believed was physically possible; that he could survive trials that were far beyond his imagination. He would come to realize that many times it was mind over matter, or mind over body that would pull him through victoriously to the other side.

It meant giving up the son I had raised to hardships that in my mother's heart, I could not imagine my son going through. Not only physical ordeals but also verbal onslaughts that would take an unshakable emotional and psychological core to withstand, built into him over years of fierce parental love. It was very exciting and yet terrifying at the same time, for all of us.

The crazy thing about it was that this had been his dream since he turned thirteen years old. Scott had wanted to fly for as long as he could remember. Back when he was in eighth grade English class, he wrote an essay in which he stated, "I hope by the time you read this again, you'll be on your way to the United States Air Force Academy"! Then he joined the Civil Air Patrol, a USAF auxiliary organization that is much like the Boy Scouts but with an aeronautical focus, and was active until he graduated from high school. When he realized that the Air Force Academy only took the cream of the crop when it came to grades, he made it his goal to graduate, well-rounded, in the top of his class, and he pursued his congressional nominations to attend the Academy like a pit bull. We never lifted a finger to ensure he would attend college there, and when two congressional nominations came through, Scott was well on his way!

The most remarkable part of this story, in the opinion of a sappy mom, was the moment we spotted him, when we arrived in Colorado Springs at the Academy to celebrate his graduation from Basic Training. We had spoken about where to meet and tried valiantly to scour the hordes of "doolies" (freshmen) that walked by us. However, it was incredibly difficult to pick him out (or so we thought) from the other young men and women who marched proudly past us, looking handsome but remarkably similar in their uniforms.

Suddenly, there he was! We recognized his gait, but hardly him! Where our teenager had once stood, here was this young man in his dress blues, shoulders back, chin high with his Air Force hat squarely on his forehead, looking as self-confident and grown up as he ever had. We sent our boy off at the airport and he had become a man, proving what he was made of in those weeks of training and tribulation. What an amazing metamorphosis. Then again, there is just something about a man in uniform. Without a doubt, he was the most handsome young man there.

Cadet Van De Water and his brothers at the USAF Academy

HAMBURG HONEY
FROM BEN'S BEES

Eat honey, my son, for it is good;
honey from the comb is sweet to your taste.
Know also that wisdom is sweet to your soul; if you find it,
there is a future hope for you, and your hope will not be cut off.
Proverbs 24:13, 14

When Wes was in college, he worked for a commercial beekeeper. It was an unusual job but he had done an independent study on bees as a biology major and was fascinated with the whole process of beekeeping and producing honey. He had learned about how they communicate where the nectar or pollen can be found and how far away it is, by wagging their tails. Wes worked steadily for the commercial beekeeper until the day he got stung about thirty times. It was rainy that day and I have since learned that bees are ornery in rainy weather because they can't be out and about doing their business.

When Wes accepted an opportunity to work at a local greenhouse for a good friend of ours, he asked if he could also keep some beehives in the far corner of the property. Then he approached Ben to see if Ben had any interest in helping collect the honey, bottling it and selling it at the greenhouse for a little profit. Ben was game although a little reticent. The main reason for his hesitation was his paralyzing fear of bees although he had been stung only once when he was little. Quite frankly, Ben didn't even enjoy a picnic on our back patio for fear of being a target again.

His reticence only inspired Wes to order a beekeeper's outfit in Ben's size, complete with a veiled hat, gloves and full bee-proof overalls. It was the perfect thing—because it gave Ben the courage to be out among the bees, hearing the buzzing in his ears, knowing he was 99% safe. We agreed to help Ben collect the honey from the frames where the bees store it in wax honeycombs, process it in the extractor which removes the honey from the comb and bottle it in sixteen ounce bottles that read "Hamburg Honey from Ben's Bees" on a lovely oval label.

Granted, our output wasn't tremendous but there was a real sense of accomplishment when Ben sold a bottle to a customer and collected the $5.00 that he charged per sixteen ounces. Apparently, there's some strong evidence that local honey, used in tea or as sweetener in other foods, can stave off allergies from the local pollen-producing trees and shrubs. We built up some "regulars" and Ben got some pocket money and learned about budgeting, tithing and pleasing customers. It's probably not something he'll continue to do once he has left home for college, but he would be the first to tell you that it was an interesting "gig" and he never once got stung! Besides, on more than one occasion his "honey money" came in very handy. Sweet!

A LONG OVERDUE
NOTE OF THANKS

Encourage each other every day while you have the opportunity.
Hebrews 3:13

My heart is steadfast, O God, my heart is steadfast.
I will sing and make music.
Psalm 57:7

Have you ever taken the time to thank a teacher? My mom, who was an ESL (English as a Second Language) teacher, had a bumper sticker on her car that said, "If you can read this, thank a teacher!" I can attest to the fact that it means more than you'll ever know if you take the time to let a gifted teacher know the influence they have had on your child's education.

Our boys all had the same vocal music teacher in high school who began teaching there the year that our Scott entered as a freshman. We have no doubts that it was a God-thing! N.Z. was amazing, and all three of our boys benefited from his musicianship and mentoring during their four years at Hamburg High School. If you asked each of them to name who their top teachers were as far as the impact they had on their formation as young adults, N.Z. would be at the top of each list. When our Mark graduated from Ithaca College with a Music Education major, summa cum laude, and went on to teach vocal music at a central New York high school the next year, we knew he was following in N.Z.'s footsteps.

So, we took the time to write a note of appreciation for the foundation he had painstakingly laid in the lives of our boys. His love of and passion for music played out daily in his teaching and our boys were not the only ones who benefited from this man's teaching style and mentoring. His students grew to love, admire and respect him with all their hearts, as was evident to us when we enjoyed concerts there over the ten years of having students at that high school. We will miss those concerts tremendously, as they were an integral part of every season and we were always impressed with what we heard at those performances. Our boys' high school years flew by, but were marked by the highlights of their various musical endeavors throughout the years.

Wes and I have taken the word "coincidence" right out of our vocabulary because the only definition we accept for that word now is: God working anonymously. We strongly believe that it was part of God's divine design that we ended up in the school district where we did, with three young men who loved to sing and play instruments and who came from a home where music was in the very air we all breathed. All of that was nurtured during school days as they participated in musicals, chamber singers, select chorus, all-guys' ensembles and instrumental music of all types as well, from marching band to wind ensemble, orchestra and jazz ensemble.

Without a doubt, this particular teacher will always have a special place in the hearts of our entire family. He always went above and beyond, was always firm but fair, and instilled in them a love of the arts.

In conclusion, let a teacher know if they are doing a good job. So often, teachers only hear the complaints and the criticism. What would happen to our education system if parents turned things around and started to thank and support the teachers who work so hard during the seven hour day (which is often extended to nine or ten hours) when we entrust our children into their care? Not only are teachers grossly underpaid, but they are most definitely "under-thanked!" Not all are stellar, granted. However, those that are need to know that we notice and feel our support. We took the time to express our gratitude and N.Z. humbly thanked us for our letter and wrote that it was appreciated more than we will ever know.

So, if you have read this, thank a teacher!

THE THREE MUSKETEERS

The Importance of Brother Bonds

Be completely humble and gentle;
be patient, bearing with one another in love.
Make every effort to keep the unity of the Spirit
through the bond of peace.
Ephesians 4:2, 3

One of my favorite pictures of all three of our sons is a shot we took when we were out west visiting Scott on his graduation weekend from the Air Force Academy. We had decided to take a walk at a park called Red Rock, near The Garden of the Gods, that is wooded with a reservoir and has some of the spectacular red rock formations that Colorado is named for.

Wes and I were lagging a little behind our guys, enjoying watching the camaraderie as the three brothers sauntered along, carrying on a lighthearted conversation and occasionally punching one another or pushing each other over. Wes called out to them to turn around and face us and snapped yet another photo. They were a little perturbed because we had been taking their pictures constantly during the visit, enjoying our time with the three, well aware of the fact that Scott would be leaving us to fly before we knew it. There they were, lined up across the road, each in their own characteristic stance but looking very much like the three musketeers with their attitudes of: "all for one and one for all." When we developed the picture (back before the digital age of cameras) we agreed that the photo could have had a caption that read, "You mess with my brother, you're going to have to mess with me!"

As parents, we kind of fumbled onto a family rule: "always look out for each other as brothers and always respect the bond between you." That didn't mean that they didn't fight with one another. They did! Ben, being the pesky littlest brother with a five-and-a-half year gap in age was always the odd man out. However, I can truthfully say that it was never malicious or nasty. We discouraged malevolent interaction and reminded them of the importance of their relationship. When push came to shove, they knew that their brothers had their backs, and now there is no doubt that they would do anything for each other if ever a call came. It is a good feeling; it gives them all a sense of confidence and comfort.

It was also interesting that when Scott got married, he made a pact with Mark and Ben. Scott asked Mark to be his best man, Mark asked Ben and Ben will have Scott as his best man when his wedding day comes. "All for one and one for all!" It is a triangle of strength and brotherhood that we cherish and hope will be intact for as long as they live.

"You mess with my
brother, you're going to
have to mess with me!"

The three musketeers
yucking it up!

ADVICE FROM THE BROS—
NEVER DRIVE WITH MOM

"Never lend your car to anyone to whom you have given birth!"
Erma Bombeck

You haven't earned your parent badge unless you have lived through the driver education phase of parenting teenagers!

I always considered myself a relatively calm, level headed, patient person. If you polled my family, however, you may get an entirely different point of view. Once our boys turned sixteen and started begging to take drivers education and get their permits, I suddenly realized just how skittish and paranoid I could be. Each of our boys had the wonderful experience of driving with mom when they were first learning and finding out how terrified I was of dying in a car accident.

Once our oldest got his license, the advice started to trickle down through the ranks: never drive with Mom if you can help it! They became acutely aware of the motions I made, though involuntary, as they drove tentatively down our neighborhood streets. It didn't take much for me to gasp, moan, inhale audibly through clenched teeth, press the invisible brake pedal on the passenger side of the van, or grip the dashboard when they were practicing. Have you ever wondered why it's called the "dashboard"? In my defense, I never screamed or yelled at them but I guess the white, waxy pallor on my face as I got out when the ordeal was over, was enough to let them know that their driving still needed some work!

By the time Ben was sixteen, the word was out and he rarely asked to go driving with me. I really couldn't understand it, since I was a seasoned passenger by then, having survived a parking job in our church parking lot, which found us ramming a cement stanchion. Okay Scott...I won't mention names, however, *someone* put the car into drive instead of reverse after successfully pulling headlong into a space by a light pole. Honestly, I had a hard time just being in the back seat as Wes sat cool as a cucumber up in front in the passenger seat. I suppose they could still hear my sudden inhalations.

Ben gave me a Mother's Day card right around that time which showed a Mom in the passenger seat of a car driven by her teenage son. Her arm is stretched out straight in front of her boy and her face shows pure terror. The inside says, "Happy Mother's Day to Mom—the original seat belt." Amen!

I really have nothing to gripe about since it took *me* three times to finally pass *my* driver's test. The first time I took the road test, I was so nervous that I got out of the car while it was still in drive. The examiner jumped behind the wheel, and announced out the open window in an unbelievably calm voice that I had failed. I could hear my own mom sigh with relief, as the roads had just become a bit safer for the next few months while I continued to practice my pathetic driving skills.

I am sure there is a very special place in heaven for road test examiners. It's a miracle more of them don't get there before their time!

MEASURING UP

Do not withhold good from those who deserve it,
when it is in your power to act.
Proverbs 3:27

My son, pay attention to what I say; listen closely to my words.
Do not let them out of your sight, keep them within your heart;
for they are life to those who find them
and health to a man's whole body.
Above all else, guard your heart, for it is the wellspring of life.
Proverbs 5:20-23

"I don't think I ever measure up!"

No seven words have pierced my heart as much as these, spoken by our middle son Mark. I was flabbergasted and devastated! He was talented, handsome, funny, intelligent, popular, loving, caring and faith-filled. Yet, as he admitted these feelings from deep in his heart at the kitchen table one afternoon, he had tears in his eyes. It broke my heart to hear him confide in this way, for my initial response was that somehow we had inadvertently made him feel inferior, inadequate or less loved than his brothers and we were sick at the thought. It would haunt me for months as I racked my brain to find something we may have said or done to give him these feelings of mediocrity.

As a middle child myself, following in the very accomplished footsteps of my older brother, I could totally relate. How often had I spent my days striving to measure up to *my* big brother who was captain of the football team, president of his class and an all-around great, popular guy? I could only imagine that those sentiments played in Mark's mind to undermine his self-confidence and self-worth. As I listened, and remembered having the same heart-wrenching feelings, I heard myself asking Mark, "But why? How can you say that? You have so much going for you! Look at everything you have done and all the wonderful things ahead of you. You have so much potential and you have already accomplished so much. How can you possibly feel that you don't measure up? We are so proud of you and love you so much!"

I have to admit - it must have been difficult, following in his older brother's shadow, when Scott seemed to have the Midas touch. Everything he went for in life was his: top grades, sports accolades, musical leads, senatorial nominations and an acceptance to the Air Force Academy. He probably seemed like the "golden boy" in our eyes to Mark. Had we not let Mark see that, without a doubt, he too had the Midas touch? As parents, we had to focus on hearing what Mark wasn't saying!

As a parent, I really have to say that I love each of my children equally. They are all precious and bring such different things to life. Each of them is special and unique and I love all three of our boys for who they are, not what they do or accomplish. Mark, Ben and Scott are similar in many ways and very different in other ways.

I found some solace in a book entitled *The Birth Order Book* by Kevin Leman. In it, Dr. Leman describes the middle child as often relegated to the background, feeling out of place, misunderstood, bypassed or upstaged at home by siblings older and younger than themselves. They have a deep need to belong and often have feelings of rejection and being the fifth wheel. The good news is that middle children, according to Dr. Leman, tend to be most faithful in marriages, loyal and prone to stick to commitments. He was accurate when it came to me, was he with Mark?

Fortunately, despite the fact Leman claims that middle children tend to be a closed book and secretive with their feelings, playing it close to the chest with relationships, we were grateful that Mark was able to express himself on such a deep, emotional level and admit these feelings, although they were tough for us to hear. He was always the guy who seemed to take things in stride, fairly even keeled, never letting situations bother him for too long. Maybe we were wrong. We came to understand that Mark wasn't always able to share how he really felt about things and we realized that we hadn't taken the time to really talk, feel him out and make him feel special. Life was a breeze for him thanks to Mark's unbelievably great sense of humor. There were no giant mountains or plunging valleys in his life, or so it appeared! He was so easy-going that we skated along beside him without worrying about him too much. This admission on his part was like a bomb, dropped in the middle of our skating party.

If anything, it reminded us of the age-old saying, "still waters run deep." You can't always trust what you see on the surface to be the whole story. We neglected to take the time to really know what Mark was thinking and how he was feeling. We dealt with the tip of the iceberg when we saw it, but never looked down under the surface until the bomb was dropped and we were forced to open our eyes. Thankfully, after several good talks, we felt that he regained his sense of self-worth and will continue to feel our unconditional love his whole life.

Mark, you'll always be the middle born, but never, ever mediocre in our eyes! You too have the Midas touch. Thanks for being candid with us. Throw away that measuring stick and stand tall!

NO THANK YOU TV

A word aptly spoken is like apples of gold in settings of silver.
Proverbs 25:11

For these commands are a lamp, this teaching is a light;
and the corrections of discipline are the way of life.
Proverbs 6:23

Our boys used to mock me mercilessly about a phrase I used pretty regularly regarding the kind of shows that became prevalent on TV as they were getting older. Of course, they watched their fair share of Barney (the talking, dancing purple dinosaur) as they were growing up, as well as *Thunder Cats, Power Rangers* and *GI Joe* — the last three being borderline as far as I was concerned regarding the level of violence. *Sesame Street* was by far the favorite with all the music and educational value, as well as a show named *Reading Rainbow*. Then there were the cute ones: I didn't have any complaints against *Hey Arnold* and

Sponge Bob Squarepants. Of course, we never tired of the Disney musicals even as adults!

However, when something was advertised that, in my opinion, had way too much "questionable" content (language, sexual innuendos, disrespect of either authority figures or women, over the edge violence, or the things that nightmares are made of), I often, without even realizing it at first, would cross my arms and very loudly exclaim, "No thank you!" The boys came to understand that my gestures and words meant that there was no way that particular program was being aired in our home on my watch. It became increasingly difficult to find things that were appropriate and so we ended up signing up for a wholesome video subscription called *Feature Films for the Family* which sent family videos that were guaranteed to not have any questionable content. We have them to this day, though we don't even own a VHS player anymore. It is so hard to throw out things that hold memories of laughter and fun, family time together.

As so often happens, our older boys came home from college and bitterly complained that we were allowing Ben to watch programs we strictly prohibited when they were still living at home. It is interesting how the rules change as you get older and realize that if you've laid a firm foundation, you can relax a little more!

It's a tricky balancing act to juggle what they can handle and when. We used to think we should shield them when they were little from things like bad language, and then they would come home reporting the new word they had learned on the school bus! I guess it's far better to subject them to reality, and teach them how to navigate in the big, sometimes bad world. So we're back to the "no-thank-you" helping! Just a little of the disagreeable stuff, please.

THE SUPERMARKET FLYER AD
IN SONG AND SPANGLISH
TO MAKE US CRINGE

Then I commend the enjoyment of life,
because nothing is better for a man under the sun
than to eat and drink and be glad.
Then joy will accompany him in his work
all the days of the life God has given him under the sun.
Ecclesiastes 8:15

Sing to the Lord a new song for he has done marvelous things.
Psalm 98:1a

B en has always been known for being musically inclined. He's off to Ithaca College to major in composition after an elementary to high school history loaded with musical experiences that started in kindergarten and will undoubtedly continue throughout his life.

Our youngest eats, sleeps and breathes eighth note runs, drum rhythms, keyboard riffs, trumpet jazz improvisations and saxophone cadenzas. After busy days traveling with the family on vacations or pole vaulting for track after school, he often runs upstairs and sequesters himself in his bedroom to "download" his latest composition from his brain into Sibelius, his computer composing software.

We didn't realize how bad it had gotten until the day that we were dropping him off for a late afternoon commitment at the high school and pulled out of the driveway, stopping quickly to collect the mail out of our mailbox. There in the pile was a supermarket ad flyer. The trip to Hamburg High was hilarious and memorable as Ben was soon singing all about the week's specials for produce, meat, deli and just about everything in the store flyer in jazz, bebop, Broadway, opera and blues styles. He's got it *bad*!

The composing bug has bitten him — or rather God has truly gifted him. We expect great things as Ben continues to explore his musical talents. We just never knew when he would break into song and crack us up! We miss him, not least because shopping at our supermarket has become so boring!

Another very unusual talent that Ben has is the ability to turn any word into a Spanish-sounding translation. He took three years of Spanish in high school and finally had enough by his senior year. His schedule was packed full and so he opted to drop the last year of study. However his foundation gave him plenty of knowledge of Spanish and whenever he was switching into Spanish to add some flavor to a conversation, if he didn't know a word, no "problemo"! He would just add an "o" on the end or -ito and make the word sound Spanish. It was very humorous and always had the family rolling their eyes as he butchered the foreign language to the point of unrecognizable. Being proficient in the language myself, it was almost painful to listen to, but never failed to garner a smirk or groan as I prepared dinner or we sat to eat as a family. It was especially lively on TACO night. Olé!

TAKE IT ALL IN BEFORE
THEY'RE ALL GONE

We loved you so much that we delighted to share with you
not only the gospel of God but our lives as well,
because you had become so dear to us...
For you know that we dealt with each of you
as a father deals with his own children,
encouraging, comforting and urging you to live lives
worthy of God, who calls you into His kingdom and glory.
1 Thessalonians 2:8, 11

When we were younger and before we had children, we would often hear people say, "You don't realize how fast time flies until you have children!" You know what? They were right.

Maybe its because the days are measured first in diaper changes and feedings, then school times, bus schedules and after school activities, then sports seasons, concerts, and exams on the calendar, then college application deadlines and finally, holidays when they come home from college. It does indeed go by in the blink of an eye it seems and before you know it, the house is empty and you're waiting for the phone to ring so you can hear their voice and make sure that life is treating them well in your absence.

One thing we thought to do which ended up being a treasure and a tradition was saving each son's thirteen years of school in a file and then preserving those memoirs in a four-inch binder.

I don't remember who thought to even start it, but once we did, it became an obsession and quite honestly, we got better at it with each son. Consequently, Ben's binders are by far the most complete. He ended up with two huge four-inch notebooks!

As the boys were going through their school years, we made it a habit to collect every concert program, report card, sports team picture, newspaper article, show ticket stub, writer of the month award, honor roll certificate, you name it! Anything and everything that had the Van De Water name printed on it went into a file as they skipped merrily through their school experiences. We collected pounds of paper that represented every effort they made to glean the most out of their educations. We tried to keep them in some chronological order by filing the latest event in the back of the folder.

Every letter that came home, every progress report, any programs that listed the songs they did at their concerts and the groups that they performed in went into their folder—whole forests were destroyed to add to the collection that each now has to reflect his hard work in school. Before each son's graduation party, I spent hours collating all the different tidbits of his life and trying valiantly to make sure they had been filed in chronological order. I placed it all in mylar sleeves and put them into binders to commemorate the things they loved being involved in from kindergarten through senior year. What a memento!

It was amazing to leaf through each of their binders before presenting them as graduation gifts. They start with birth certificates or sonogram pictures or perhaps a print of their tiny newborn feet that hospitals provide before you take your new baby home. Then there are the class photos sprinkled here and there as they grew up and their faces and bodies changed and matured. The candids from the musicals they were in and pictures of the sports teams they played on have all become precious treasures that depict their younger years and remind us the countless hours we spent as spectators, cheerleaders and audience members.

What is so astounding to me is how quickly we forgot the minute particulars. We would turn the page and gasp as we admitted, "Wow! I had totally forgotten that you did that! Unbelievable! I don't remember you winning this award!" The years tend to dull our memories and only the really remarkable highlights stand out in vivid color and detail. The other minutiae blur into months and years of flurry and activity.

When the boys got into middle school and high school and started having crazy, hard to track schedules, we bought a giant calendar to hang on our kitchen wall. It was two feet high by three feet long and had blocks that were four inch squares for each day's commitments. We started writing down all their activities: instrumental lessons, music concerts, after school or before school meetings, musical rehearsals, track, wrestling, baseball or soccer practices, dances, proms, graduations, etc., on this monster calendar. It was the only way we could stay organized. There was always a lot going on with three active, intelligent, musical guys who loved to be involved and challenged. Each had his own color wet-erase marker to keep track of his commitments and if we missed something when they were in senior high, it was on their shoulders. It's a good thing—looking back, that we had only three children. Otherwise I'd be in the loony bin by now!

We tried to stay involved…from mom accompanying their concerts and choreographing their musicals, to dad dissecting deer hearts in science and coaching soccer. Wes and I couldn't get enough of being engaged in their lives and we hope it laid a foundation for connection in their adult lives and the lives of their children as well.

When I was in high school, I remember a cheer we used to do at football games. It spelled, "b-e-a-g-g-r-e-s-s-i-v-e!" Be aggressive! Our cheer as parents became "Be engaged"—b-e-e-n-g-a-g-e-d! Engaged" and involved in the lives of our kids: because you don't realize how fast time flies. Our motto was: take it all in before they're all gone —we know we'll never regret it!

FEAR FACTOR IN REAL LIFE

Cast all your anxiety on Him because He cares for you.
1 Peter 5:7

'm not quite sure how God decides what our individual make-up will be: our personality, our interests, what our experiences will be and our qualifications later in life to pursue the unique hopes and dreams that we hold in our hearts. I also wonder whether He determines our phobias, or whether those are instilled in us as time and life go on. All I know is that we all have them; phobias that we wouldn't choose to embrace but which definitely play a part in how we approach life and how we respond or react to our circumstances. Webster quotes that a phobia is defined as an irrational, intense and persistent fear of certain situations, activities, things, animals or people. It causes anxiety and the intense drive to avoid the feared stimulus.

For example, I know that I exhibited an extreme phobia of heights at a very early age (maybe a few weeks old). When I was older I was told that, though most babies laugh and enjoy being tossed in the air and caught, my tiny body grew instantly rigid and tense when I was lifted above someone's head. It was not a fun thing for me as an infant or toddler and this particular fear of heights continues to plague me even as an adult. I can't walk over subway gratings without getting what feels like an electric jolt in my legs. I hate bridges, high buildings, roller coasters, ravines, gorges and waterfalls (which is unfortunate, living forty-five minutes from Niagara Falls, considered one of this world's most spectacular wonders.)

Our sons each had things that made them very nervous and some of these phobias were kept relatively secret. I never realized, for instance, that our middle son Mark had a deep-seated fear of being left behind somewhere or abandoned. It may have taken root in the retelling of the following story: my family was traveling cross-country one summer when I was in middle school, camping all the way from Long Island, New York to Seattle, Washington where my cousins lived. We enjoyed all the national landmarks along the way despite being packed snuggly into a station wagon, including our family mutt, Merfi. Obviously, we stopped many times over the approximately three thousand miles for potty breaks.

At one point, we all climbed out at a gas station, filled the tank, took our turns in the restrooms, climbed back in and headed off. About ten minutes down the road, I perked up, taking my nose out of the latest romance novel I was reading, and noticed that my sister was not in the car. I spoke up, only to have the family laugh it off as a joke. "I'm not kidding!" I shrieked. My father trounced on the brake, turned around and with horror, realized that I was indeed telling the truth. We roared back to the gas station to find my sister sobbing her eyes out on the curb, sure that we had left her there forever!

I guess that story must have impressed our Mark. He held this fear for most of his growing up years, much to my surprise and consternation. We just recently learned of it. Talk about "leaving your Mark"! That's exactly what he was afraid of all along.

Our Ben is afraid of bees — he's better now but that phobia is the topic of the previous chapter entitled, "Hamburg Honey from Ben's Bees." I doubt he's considering beekeeping as a lifelong hobby.

My husband is claustrophobic. For anyone who can relate to this particular fear, it can be suffocating to experience the symptoms brought on by an enclosed space. Even if that tight space can offer vital medical information (like an MRI machine) for someone like Wes, it's out of the question.

One of our guys experiences skin-crawling fear when he sees a snake. I can personally relate to that fear when it comes to arachnids. I don't care how itsy bitsy the spider is, I am paralyzed and cannot bring myself to get near it. Yet I can hold a snake, no problem. It is truly fascinating. Neither of us has ever had a life-threatening experience with either of these creatures and yet, the hair on our necks stands on end in their presence when they slither or crawl into our immediate surroundings. Another one of our guys went through a phase of being terrified that our house would be broken into by robbers or that we would suffer the tragedy of a house fire. When he was younger, he spent many-a-night on our bedroom floor, being too afraid to sleep in his own room. My husband and I were robbed once in Miami, Florida before we had kids, and maybe the retelling of that story stuck. Children are so impressionable. You never know what will affect them and how.

Phobias — We all have them. We can't deny them. They are real, even if irrational. We can brush something off as an adult and never realize that it has taken root in our child as an irrational fear that will become debilitating over time.

If the Van De Water family was crammed into a tiny room, a hundred stories up with a glass floor that was filled with bees and snakes, and then left there indefinitely — that would be the end of us! Sounds like "Fear Factor" reality TV to me!

SOMETIMES THE NO IS AS IMPORTANT AS THE YES

The Lord will fulfill his purpose for me;
Your love, O Lord, endures forever.
Psalm 138:8

"The man who is born with a talent which he is meant to use
finds his greatest happiness in using it."
Johann Wolfgang Von Goethe

There are different kinds of gifts, but the same Spirit.
There are different kinds of service, but the same Lord.
1 Corinthians 12:4, 5

s it me, or do others out there think that our society is making a huge mistake by requiring an eighteen year old to know exactly what path he wants to pursue in life? Colleges expect high school seniors to state their intended major on their applications before they have had any chance whatsoever to explore all the wonderful opportunities available in the expansive world of potential careers. What's the big idea? Back when Wes and I were attending college, we were expected to declare a major by our junior year. That enabled us to get some general education courses under our belts and discover where our interests lay and how our giftedness would play into our life choices. We got to search our hearts, our interests and our talents.

Certainly not every high school senior is equipped to know exactly what they would love to do for the rest of their life. (I still don't know what I want to be when I grow up!) Our Mark was an exceptional Math student as well as a gifted artist. That's why he searched for and chose a university nearby known for its architecture program. He was promptly accepted and began his freshman year with enthusiasm. It wasn't long before he realized that architecture was not his thing. Mark came to recognize the fact that he wasn't passionate enough about this major to be struggling with only two hours of sleep after working on an exceptionally difficult project that was summarily dismissed by his professor as unacceptable. It was a brutal program and soon a discouraged Mark informed us of his intentions to change majors before the semester ended.

Once he declared music as his intended path of study, we saw a remarkable change in our son. Mark was healthier, happier, and so much more himself than we had seen in the months preceding the change. We had always assumed he would do something with music, but had not wanted to interfere with his choice to fulfill his dreams of a career in architecture. We silently expressed relief as parents when we saw our son blossom in his giftedness and claim a career that fit who he was. He has achieved so much in just one short year as a choral music teacher and we know he has found his "sweet spot" — exactly where God wants him!

For Mark, the no was as important as the yes, because he could have spent much of his life looking back, wondering if he could have been happy as an architect. His bookshelves hold hardcover books of the work of Frank Lloyd Wright and his dream to someday build a house of his own may yet come true. In the meantime, he will fulfill his new dream: sharing his passions and making music come alive in his students' hearts. We're so proud of him and get to enjoy his conducting as his most admiring groupies. I get to enjoy his conducting as his accompanist! I'm honored and I love it!

Yes! Yes! Yes!

HUGS AT THE KITCHEN SINK

never thought it would be possible to miss someone enough as to actually "feel" something they did regularly even when they aren't around anymore, but it is! When Scott was at the Air Force Academy, he used to come up behind me on the rare occasion when he was home and hug me. It would be a huge bear hug that sometimes lifted me off my feet, even though he isn't a bear of a guy. He stands just six feet tall but is lean and muscular from all his physical training.

Then came the bittersweet day when we would have to send him back and we tearfully waved as he walked toward his gate at the airport, headed back again to Colorado Springs. It was never easy since the visits were so infrequent. It has gotten even harder, since he lives on the southern edge of the continental United States and we live near the top edge and our visits are fit in among hectic schedules and commitments on both sides. When deployed, he can seldom communicate with us. We know God holds him, and his wife Barbara, in the palm of His hand and loves them both even more than we do!

Scott would call when he was in pilot training and when I answered the phone I'd hear, "Hey lady!" It became his trademark greeting for me, another sweet memory. Now he mostly says, "Hey Mom" but his voice drops tenderly as the name Mom escapes his lips and I can hear the love and treasure the phone calls. I always have a hard time hanging up and I swear I can still "feel" the hugs.

On the flip side, Mark is hilarious! When *he* calls, he leaves messages like "Somebody answer the phone!" (in a squeaky, desperate voice) or "Please to call me back, yes" (in broken English). His sense of humor is the spice of life. He has the most amazing ability to change his voice or talk in foreign accents that have us rolling. Mark has many friends because he is so amusing to be around and makes the dullest event fun. He is definitely the guy to invite to a party. His messages touch our funny bones as well as our hearts.

We can "hear" Ben's smile when he calls and I always love his endearing chuckle over the phone which he does throughout our phone conversations. I miss his presence here at home terribly, since we had five and a half years of Ben by himself, with the gap in age between him and Mark.

I have seven messages from our sons on the answering machine that date at least a year back. I won't erase them! I won't, I won't, I can't!

Life is never dull when you have a sense of humor!

A RING BOUQUET AT SUNRISE
AND I LOVE YOU BECAUSE...

For I know the plans I have for you, declares the Lord,
plans to prosper you and not to harm you,
plans to give you hope and a future.
Jeremiah 29:11

One of the many things our sons have all learned from their father is how to treat a woman right and how romance can make all the difference. Both of our now-married sons proposed to their sweethearts in ways that could be recorded in the best written romance novels of the modern age — in the humble and totally unbiased opinion of their mother. Both of their strategies obviously worked and are enough to bring tears to my eyes when I think about them. Beautiful Barbara and lovely Lael are now my daughters of the heart and I love them both as if they were my own.

Scott was living in Colorado Springs near the US Air Force Academy at the time as Barbara was finishing up her "firstie" year of academics and setting her sights on graduation. They had known each other for about three years, dating off and on as their months at the USAF Academy stretched on.

The morning Scott decided to propose, he appeared in her dorm room before dawn with a gorgeous bouquet of flowers, woke Barbara up and finally convinced her, after much reluctance at that ungodly hour, to put on her coat and follow him to his car. She was still in her pajamas but made her somnambulate way to his Saturn Ion, holding the fragrant bouquet precariously in her arms. Little did she know that tied to the blooms was the engagement ring that Scott had chosen for her. He also had taken the time to write her a beautiful love poem.

They drove up to a summit in the nearby mountains of Colorado Springs where they had hiked sometime earlier in their courtship and Scott parked the car. Then as Barbara giggled uncontrollably, realization dawning on her sleepy brain as the sun rose over the mountain peaks, Scott got down on one knee, read the poem and proposed to his sweetheart. She said yes and the rest is history.

She still had to attend classes that morning and the most hilarious part of the story was when one of her professors at the Academy noticed how alert and vivacious she was that morning and commented: "Why Barbara, you're engaged this morning!" It took a while for her to regain her composure and explain why she broke out in peals of laughter at his comment. How ironic that he chose those words!

It has been hard to be so far away from our new daughter. She was stationed in Germany for two years and is now spending one more year overseas before returning home, we hope, for good. Our relationship with her, getting to know her well and being able to be involved in their lives is temporarily on hold. Furthermore, we wait with anticipation for the day when she is finally close to us in every way, not only in spirit! She and Scott have always been in our hearts and on our minds, and certainly in our prayers as they fight to preserve the freedoms we all enjoy in this incredible country.

Now for Mark's story: he fell in love with lovely Lael at college as well. They both love music and their paths crossed regularly as they each pursued their music education degrees. At Christmas in 2009 he approached us to see what we thought about his proposing to Lael on

New Year's Eve. What a lovely time to look to the future and imagine a life together with your one and only. We were thrilled!

Mark ordered an engagement ring which he designed himself and decided that he needed a distraction from the real deal. We agreed that Mark would give Lael a pair of pearl earrings pretending they were from him. When she opened them, she was thrown off of the thought that maybe, just maybe, he would be presenting her with an engagement ring. They enjoyed a romantic dinner for two at a restaurant and then exchanged Christmas gifts back at Lael's apartment.

The night before, Mark had stayed awake until 5:00 am, preparing a special leather bound booklet for his proposal. The gist of it was "I Love You Because…" and it was filled with his thoughts about why and how he loved Lael; things like "I love you because of the way you treat people, I love you because you are so beautiful, I love you because you help me want to be a better person, I love you because you make me want to spend the rest of my life with you!" He included pictures of their courtship with every sentiment and presented it to her as a prelude to his proposal. When she got to the last page he proposed, and she flew into his arms crying, "Yes, yes, yes!" and didn't even wait to see the ring!

We were privileged to tearfully share Mark's precious handmade treasure when they visited us after New Year's Eve. It was a tender moment for Wes and me as we got a glimpse into the two loving hearts of this beautiful couple who would soon be intimately tied together as part of this family. We rejoice with them in the blessing that is God's gift of love!

What more could we wish for as parents? Two lovely daughters who will love our sons as much as we love them both; sweet, beautiful, intelligent, strong yet compassionate women who will respect our young men for who they are and in return, receive loyal, fierce love for a lifetime. What a joy! We wonder who God has planned for our Ben and we can't wait to meet her, embrace her and welcome her into our family.

IN THREE WEEKS,
IN CALIFORNIA,
GO BUY A DRESS

"After the initial pain of releasing our children,
there comes joy and peace, both for them and us,
because we know that no matter what stage of life our children are in,
when we release them to God, they are in good hands!"
Stormie O'Martian

t was January 3, 2007, when the phone rang and our son Scott said happily to us, "What would you think if Barbara and I got married?" "Wonderful! That's great!" we responded. "What year? What month?"

"This year, this month — in three weeks, on January 19 in California! Go buy a dress and get your airline tickets soon!"

Oh my goodness, what a whirlwind! Scott and Barbara had postponed their wedding the summer before after planning the ceremony for the week after Barbara graduated from the Air Force Academy. That was a good decision because in retrospect, it would have been chaotic to pull it off, trying to plan a wedding as she finished up her senior year at the academy. We were grateful that they didn't try getting it all organized then, but were caught totally off guard when they called on January 3. They had spent the holidays with us and had just left Buffalo a few days before. Never once, during their week here in Western New York had they mentioned a wedding. However, when we realized their reason for the rush, it made sense.

It turned out that Barbara was to be deployed in February, just weeks after their truncated honeymoon of two days in Napa Valley. It made all the sense in the world for them to marry before her deployment because it would ensure their placement together once that requirement was fulfilled (or so we thought)! The gown which she had bought in anticipation of the summer wedding was called into play in January. They quickly arranged for a reception at Barbara's Air Force base in California, placed an order with a bakery for a gorgeous wedding cake adorned with roses and lilies, and pulled together their wedding party of brothers, sisters and cousins. Wes and I were honored to be asked to sing one of our favorite romantic songs by Steven Curtis Chapman entitled, *I Will Be Here* and off we went to California, minus any other relatives or family on such short notice. They even managed to reserve six USAF airmen, dapper in their dress-blue uniforms, to form an arch with their sabers over the newlyweds on their way out of the base chapel. The wedding cake topper was an Air Force Lieutenant and his bride, acquired on E-Bay by our industrious son.

The whole affair was simply amazing! Leave it to two officers in the United States Air Force to pull off such an incredible event in three weeks time. We were totally blown away. We met Barbara's family for the first time the night of the rehearsal dinner and truly enjoyed our evening getting to know them as best we could. It was probably one of the most whirlwind experiences that Wes and I have ever had in our lifetime. Nevertheless, God's blessing was on them. Everything fell into place beautifully and we came away with special memories that we will treasure forever.

One memory that I will forever hold dear was the Mother/Son dance with my eldest at the reception. How bittersweet it was as I held this young man in my arms whom I birthed into the world, so handsome in his military uniform on his wedding day. He seemed taller than ever, proud as punch as he glanced intermittently at his beautiful bride, and yet, his chubby little face as a toddler flitted across my mind as I struggled with the thought of letting go. That is our job, after all. We must give them roots, and in his case, quite literally, wings. I have often heard the rhyme, "A daughter's a daughter all of her life; a son is a son until he chooses a wife." However, I will do everything in my power to gain a daughter rather than lose a son. We are taking baby steps toward that end as we speak. She is so precious to my heart, and Scott was the first son to make me a mom.

The song he chose for our dance was *It Had To Be You*, an oldie goldie that is frequently requested at the nursing homes and assisted living centers where I play the piano and sing for the residents. I have since teased that the following two lines of the song inspired this precious groom to make that particular choice: "Some others I've seen, might never be mean, might never be cross or try to be boss, but they wouldn't do." I know there were times as I look back that I may have won the "meanest" mother on the block award for my strict parenting style, but look at the result. I could never be prouder of the man he has become and the woman he has chosen as his soul mate.

The song continues: "with all your faults, I love you still...it had to be you!" We all have our faults. I didn't do everything right. I was new at the mothering thing with Scott. Besides, firstborns are always the guinea pigs. Regardless, I wouldn't trade any of it for anything. I'm just grateful he loves me still!

Air Force Lieutenants who pulled off an incredible wedding in just 3 weeks!

ALL I WANT IS LOVING YOU
AND MUSIC, MUSIC, MUSIC

The Reprise

And I pray that you, being rooted and established in love,
may have power, together with all the saints,
to grasp how wide and long and high and deep is the love of Christ.
Ephesians 3:17b-18

We heard it repeatedly: "That was the best wedding I ever attended!"

What an incredible, gorgeous day! Mark and Lael were married on July 11, 2010, at the Hilltop Restaurant in Elmira, New York and we couldn't have asked for better weather. It had been swelteringly hot the week before, but the humidity broke and all we had were blue skies and sunshine, not to mention, such a breathtaking spot. The restaurant overlooks a gorgeous valley and the view is spectacular. Our hearts quivered with great expectations.

The afternoon and evening were seamless from beginning to end. They planned the ceremony under a big tent on a cement platform outside. The white chairs were set in two sections with a wide aisle down the middle. The pastor who married them stood with Mark and Ben, his best man, waiting up at the front. There's a picture of everyone watching the bride come up the center aisle, except Wes and me. We were watching our son as his lovely Lael came into view. It was all he could do not to weep as his wife-to-be walked towards him. Our hearts overflowed.

The ceremony was precious. The bride and groom started it all out by presenting white roses to their moms and hugging their Dads to say thanks for their nurturing foundations and the love that was in their homes as they grew up, found one another and fell in love. Our hearts were touched.

The pastor who married them said that normally he would admonish the couple to do this and that, and not forget such and such, but that Lael and Mark already had so much going for them; most importantly-strong faiths in God. Their marriage was being built with God at the center of the union. What parent could ask for more? Our hearts rejoiced.

After the beautiful ceremony, which included a flute and keyboard duet as well as a choir piece, performed by twenty talented friends from Ithaca College's School of Music (Lael and Mark's alma mater) everyone moved into the restaurant for hors d'oeuvres and drinks as the photographer took hundreds of pictures of the gorgeous couple, their bridal party and relatives. She was very creative and our hearts were tickled pink.

During the reception Mark and Lael had everyone stand and sing a song containing the word "love" to make them kiss, in lieu of tinkling our glasses with our silverware. With the musical talent represented in the room it was really fun. Mark even serenaded his new wife with some college friends who were members with Mark of an a cappella group at Ithaca and that was also truly memorable. Our hearts fluttered with romance.

Ben's best man speech was aided by a two-foot-tall wine glass. He quipped that the couple was so exceptional that only a toast that big would suffice. The reception hall erupted with applause and our hearts jiggled with joy.

The reception indoors was followed by dessert and dancing out on a patio under the stars, featuring the father-bride and mother-groom dances. Lael danced with her dad to *How Sweet It Is to be Loved by You* by the ever-popular James Taylor, which had the whole crowd clapping and singing along. My precious son asked *me* to pick our song. I couldn't think of a better one than Mark Harris' ballad, *Find Your Wings*. As we started and my Mark heard the words wafting over the cool summer breeze, his eyes teared and he said, "You had to pick this one?" Yes, I had to pick that one. Buy Mark Harris' CD, listen to the lyrics and you'll understand why. I was told there wasn't a dry eye on the patio. I wouldn't know…my eyes were focused on my handsome son, now a husband, looking forward to a life of love and commitment with his new bride. My heart burst with love and pride.

We successfully launched our second into the arms of a sweet, lovely young woman who loves our son dearly. Our hearts are at peace.

The Prince and his Princess

Too cute: they are perfect for each other

We are two-thirds of the way to gaining three treasured daughters-of-the-heart, with two beautiful daughters-in-law already in the fold. God has a plan for Ben, we have no doubt about that, and so, we know we will love our third daughter as well. Furthermore, Wes and I wouldn't miss the next wonderful season of being grandparents for the world. We want to be as fully involved with our sons' families and in their lives as they wish us to be. Our hearts wait in anticipation.

'All I want is loving you and music, music, music' — is there anything better in life? Love and music! They make our world go 'round. I can't imagine life without either one of them. Harmony — that's what I'm talking about! Our hearts are full.

UTERUS-LESS IN BUFFALO

The Finality of It All

In the morning, O Lord, You hear my voice.
In the morning, I lay my requests before You
and wait in expectation.
Psalm 5:3

I lift up my eyes to the hills—where does my help come from?
My help comes from the Lord, the Maker of heaven and earth.
Psalm 121:1, 2

was truly on the verge of panic. My guess is that many pre-op patients get like that at the last minute, ready to launch straight off their gurney and run down the hospital hallway in their not-so-discreet hospital gown screaming, "Get me out of here, I've changed my mind and I don't want to go through with it!" I felt incredibly vulnerable, being totally nude under the pathetic paper gown which I'm convinced they make you wear so you'll stay put on the gurney. It was the idea of going under general anesthesia that had me so fearful. The day before my scheduled hysterectomy, someone we knew went into a coma as a result of wrongly administered drugs after coming successfully through surgery. He was still in a coma and he was still on my mind.

It wouldn't be long now. I could feel myself on the edge. God knew I was teetering and so, He sent me Lynn. At first, the pre-op nurse was very businesslike and professional, busying herself with the preparations for my hysterectomy by wrapping both my legs in massaging stockings that filled with air every now and then and kept the blood pumped up into my torso and head. I had already donned the ultra fashionable blue synthetic stretch booties with hat to match. I guess they want you looking your best, although you are required to forego makeup, hair products, jewelry or even your latest Goodwill find for two bucks which still has the original price tag from Ann Taylor.

Finally, after I was totally prepped, Lynn came to me with a clipboard and started asking the routine questions. What was my name? What was my birth date? What was my understanding of the surgery that was to be performed on me? They had to be sure that I was the right patient, undergoing the proper procedure on the correct body part. I was grateful for their persistent checking. I would have hated to come out of surgery, only to find that they had removed my appendix by accident!

Then Lynn asked, "Have you ever had major surgery before?"

All I could think of was what I was facing and so, with a totally straight face I nodded and instead of stating that I had had three C-sections, I proudly replied, "Yes, I have had three hysterectomies!"

I didn't even realize my error at first. However, Lynn was on the ball. Her eyes flew wide open and with a howl, she asked me, "Really? Was that because you had four uteruses, or was it that they just couldn't get it right and tried three times before this, to haul that sucker out of you?" Well, we started giggling, and soon it erupted into all-out guffaws. I asked her "If cows can have three stomachs, why can't I have four uteruses?" She hooted over that too and then called over another nurse who had glanced over wondering what all the fuss was about. "We've got to keep our eye on this one Rachel, she's trouble!" Tears were streaming down my cheeks by the time I calmed down. I was giddy with nerves. However, that was not the end of it.

Every time either of the two nurses went by me in their busy prepping of other patients, they would put two fingers up to their own eyes, and point to me as if to say, "We are watching you!" Fresh giggles would bubble up every time, until one of the hospital surgeons entered the pre-op area. He wasn't pleased with our shenanigans! After reprimanding poor Lynn for being "unprofessional" he focused on the patient next to me who had come in for back surgery on two ruptured discs. I felt sorry that we had carried on so, being the unintentional instigator of the hilarity. I tried valiantly to behave, but Lynn and Rachel took it with a grain of salt; motioning a zip of their lips and throw of the key whenever they caught my eye, or tiptoeing dramatically past me as if on eggshells! They were absolutely "just what the doctor ordered."

There was the expected visit from the anesthetist for my case who started the IV in my hand. Finally, I had a visit from the doctor who would be assisting my gynecologist in running the DaVinci robot that would actually perform my laparoscopic hysterectomy. When he stated "I know how to do the robot," my two cohorts in crime resorted to one last mischievous act and broke into the robot dance behind him! It was all I could do to keep a straight face. This time, it wasn't my fault.

What a gift! At a moment when I was racked with fear, God sent me laughter and humor to reassure me that He was in control. I will be forever grateful for these two nurses who put me at ease just before I was rolled down the hall for my surgery. By then, my anxiety had dissipated with all the endorphins coursing through my body.

How can I wonder if God cares for little old me? Someone could have come to hold my hand and talk gently with me about the safety of the procedure I was about to undergo. That probably would have assuaged my fears. Instead, He sent me humor in uniform—two nurses who will forever remain in my memory; two women who yucked it up with me the entire time I was in their care. I was facing major surgery to end a wonderful phase in my life of bringing children into this world. It could have been emotionally traumatic for me.

There is such finality in having a hysterectomy—it's a resonant slam of the door on the season of childbearing. Although I could never imagine being pregnant and starting this motherhood thing again at my age, there was a tinge of sadness as I stepped out of the hospital, "uterus-less in Buffalo"! I had to set my sights on being a grandmother and all the joy that will entail. It will be a new season in life, another adjustment, like that of the empty nest.

Undeniably, God is so good! He shows me every day in many ways that He is watching over me and my family. I am forever grateful for His love and care. Now that's one parent that always gets it right in the eyes of His thankful daughter.

Conclusion:

NOBODY'S PERFECT

We all stumble in many ways.
James 3:2

Love…does not boast, it is not proud.
And now these three remain: faith, hope and love.
But the greatest of these is love.
1 Corinthians 13:4b, 13

So here is the admission no one ever wants to make, especially if you are a mom like me: I wanted to be the perfect mom. I wanted to get it all right, have my act all together, raise my sons with never a worry, know I made the right decisions at the crucial moments, feel as though I disciplined correctly at every turn. That was my dream and my hope. Did it come true? No.

Our three sons would be the first to tell you that I made my fair share of mistakes. I disciplined unfairly, I refused to apologize when I should have, I was either too heavy handed or too lenient. I treated them differently in the same situations and the same in other situations when a dissimilar approach was needed. Each of our boys is unique. They required diverse mothering. I was not always on top of that or as aware as I could or should have been.

The sections in my book admitting my faults as a mom are limited, not because I did it all right, but because admitting you failed at times is a hard thing for all of us to verbalize! It is an even harder thing to confess on paper! A hard copy for posterity, yikes! It's even harder when you have a type A personality and are driven to do your best at everything. I wanted to do my best. I guess I did. However, my best wasn't perfect by any stretch of the imagination.

What I did learn was that *nobody's* perfect at this parenting thing. It is *not* for sissies! It is hard work and it takes commitment, determination and a great deal of blood, sweat and tears. Even when we've tried our best and made countless great decisions, and trained up our child in the way that he should go, life can still throw you a curve ball and shatter your dreams. How often do we hear of well-meaning, involved parents whose kids struggle, get into all kinds of terrible trouble and break their hearts?! There are no guarantees. Hindsight is always 20-20. You can look back and wish you had done this, or said that. You are sure things would have turned out differently if you had trusted your gut or taken someone's advice, but you didn't. C'est la vie. None of us are perfect, but the key is admitting it, asking forgiveness and moving on. Accepting the little you have done well is a gift and the love that you are blessed in sharing is the ultimate treasure!

Every family has its troubles. We all contribute to the "fun" in the dysfunction in our homes. There's not a family that can escape some measure of heartache. If you think you can or have, congratulations. You are in a minuscule minority. I personally think that it comes with the territory. It allows us to grow and learn to depend on God. Without Him, we're all just floundering through life. Wes and I leaned on God a great deal and quite honestly, that's what got us through. We know we couldn't have done it without a strong faith. Can anyone?

In conclusion, don't think I had it all together or got it all right. I didn't and neither will you. We will all fail our children in many ways so try to put aside that money for everyone's inevitable therapy. Just know that there are many around you, going through the same things, hurdling the same issues, dealing with the same struggles as parents. There's safety in numbers, and comfort in sharing. Reach out and learn from one another. Most of all, trust your heart and always, always lean on God! He is the only perfect parent and He wants us to have the abundant life. He knows us best because He created us, and He will guide us. Pray as you parent. To God be the glory for the things He has done!

———————

Glory belongs to God, whose power is at work in us.
By this power, He can do infinitely more
than we can ask or imagine.
Ephesians 3:20

A MOTHER'S MEMORIES

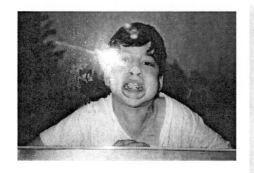

Gotta love all that orthodontic work Scott

The whole family at Busch Gardens

*A proud mom
prepares to send
her eldest off to
the USAFA*

*Scott getting ready
to rock climb*

Waiting for Christmas on the stairs - a family tradition

Still waiting for Christmas!

Mark, just hanging
out at church
during youth group

Mark — Born and Made
in the USA

Ben with his trumpet
in 4th grade

Dapper Ben

Ben finished high school swimmingly
well and headed off to college

ORDER FORM

If you would like to order more copies of this book, contact the author at her business email address: ann@annvandewater.com or contact her on her Facebook Author page:

Ann Van De Water — Author.

Also, check out Ann's **website** for more information:

www.annvandewater.com.

This book is available in major bookstores under the author's name: Ann Van De Water or the book title: **MOMMY MEMOIRS** — A Hilarious and Heartwarming Look at the Trials and Triumphs of Being a Mom, published by Morgan James Publishing, NYC. It will be available as of Nov. 2013 as an eBook and Jan./Feb. 2014 as a paperback for $17.99 plus tax and S&H.

For more information, please call the author at (716) 222-0649 and leave your contact information or mail this information card to the address above and she will contact you.

*Note that Ann is also available for speaking, consulting, and parent coaching.

CUSTOMER INFORMATION:

Name: _____

Address: _____

City:_____State: _____ Zip Code: _____

Phone #: _____ Email address: _____

**Please be aware that there will be state sales tax as well as shipping and handling fees added to your total cost. Please inquire about quantity discounts. For international shipping, contact the author directly to find out about shipping details.

CPSIA information can be obtained at www.ICGtesting.com
Printed in the USA
LVOW11s1935140214

373765LV00006B/741/P